From

DEPRESSION TO DESTINY

The Definitive Guide to Spiritual Transformation

To: Ms. Roth
Thanks for the love. God Bless

KIRK NUGENT

Copyright © 2020 by Kirk Nugent
All rights reserved. No part of this publication may be reproduced, distributed, or transmitted in any form or by any means, including photocopying, recording, or other electronic or mechanical methods, without the prior written permission of the publisher, except in the case of brief quotations embodied in critical reviews and certain other noncommercial uses permitted by copyright law.
Book Design by HMDpublishing
Published by Kirk Nugent Unlimited Global Enterprise LLC.

ACKNOWLEDGMENTS

My sincerest thanks to my Creator, you've bestowed a talent upon me and placed a passion in my heart to claim my destiny, I am indeed grateful. A special thanks to my son, JuVon. You have always believed in me and supported me throughout my darkest days. I love you relentlessly, unconditionally.

To Bhavani Lev, Bharat Mitra, Dr. Bruce Lipton, and his beloved Margaret Horton, Dr. Gladys Ato, Fay Young, Craig, and Gina Allard, Dionne Witter and the rest of my soul family: Without your unyielding love and constant support, this book would not be possible. Your love truly humbles me, and I send mine in return.

To all the people who have supported me over the years in my walk from Depression to Destiny, I love and adore you. While others had to see it, to believe it, you believed in me when there was no evidence to support your faith. From my heart to yours, I love you.

With unconditional Love, Light, and Affection, we are the ones we have been waiting for, and the Ground Crew is here and activated. Blessings.

Kirk Nugent.

FOREWORD

From Depression to Destiny by Kirk Nugent: The Background Story

The movie The Matrix is one of the most widely watched and discussed films in recent times. The story's premise is that "humanoids" (think corporations) "program" living and breathing humans to be distracted while exploiting them as power sources for the humanoids' machinery.

Cataloged as science fiction, in truth, The Matrix is a documentary! The fact that human beings are "programmed" has been known and exploited for 400 years by the Jesuits. The founders of this Order openly boasted about the power of developmental programming when they offered: "Give me a child for the first seven years, and I'll give you the man." Simply, the programs you experience as a child become the primary determinant of your fate.

Frontier Science has now revealed the biological mechanisms that substantiate this Jesuit belief. Our genes primarily serve as chemical "blueprints" used to fabricate 100,000 different proteins, the body's molecular building blocks. Genes also provide for some very basic "built-in" behavioral programs defined as "instincts," simple reflex behaviors.

The behaviors that inevitably shape our health and fate are derived from complex behavioral programs that have been downloaded into our more primitive subconscious mind. These foundational programs are acquired by simply observing the behaviors of our "teachers" - our parents, siblings, and community.

Electroencephalograph (EEG) studies reveal that a child's developing brain predominantly operates at a low vibrational frequency known as theta, an activity associated with imagination. Children under the age of seven seamlessly mix real and imaginary experiences. A broom becomes a horse, and a mud pie becomes a tea party favorite.

More importantly, theta activity induces a state of hypnosis. Consider the thousands of "rules" we must learn in order to become functional members of a family, a community, and a nation. Since civilization continuously adapts to new worlds and new world knowledge, cultural "rules" of behavior continuously evolve. Consequently, complex cultural programs/behaviors are not encoded in genes but must be learned in each generation. The juvenile brain's hypnotic theta activity enables the acquisition of this massive data dump.

Around age seven, the child's brain ramps up its vibe and predominantly operates at a higher EEG frequency, referred to as alpha-waves. Alpha activity is associated with "calm" consciousness and the experience of self-consciousness (self-awareness ... "Who am I?"). Alpha activity is associated with the nervous system's latest evolutionary advance, the "creative" conscious mind. The conscious mind, driven by imagination and reason, is the source of our wishes, desires, and aspirations.

The subconscious mind is a database of stored behavioral programs. It is the equivalent of an "auto-pilot" that controls the vehicle when the conscious mind is busy - busy thinking, imagining, and planning. Since the fundamental programs in the subconscious are derived from observing others, those behaviors do not necessarily support our wishes and desires. In fact, psychologists suggest that up to 70% or more of developmentally downloaded subconscious programs are limiting, disempowering, and self-sabotaging.

Consider the physical body as a "vehicle" and the mind as its "driver." When we operate the "vehicle" with the conscious mind, we have our hands on the wheel and are pursuing our wishes and desires on the road to "Happily Ever After."

This mechanism of manifesting life experiences emphasizes the influence of the power of positive thinking in shaping the character of our lives. I can feel what many of you are now thinking, "OH NO! Not that positive thinking stuff again! I have been thinking of all the positive things I desire in my life ... where are they?"

Neuroscience has now revealed a formerly missing piece of the "positive thinking" dilemma. Data reveals that our creative conscious minds are engaged in thought 95% of the time. While the conscious mind is in thought, our lives/behavior are still in motion. By default, our behaviors are then controlled by the programs in the auto-pilot subconscious mind. The conscious mind, being preoccupied, rarely observes our own self-sabotaging behaviors. Unfortunately, everyone else does!

Our parents and teachers unconsciously disempowered us when acting as "coaches" in shaping our behavior. Parental criticisms designed to goad us into better behavior, such as "You can do better than that!" "You don't deserve this!" "Who do you think you are?" You're not loveable!" "You're not good at that!" are not consciously understood by a child's brain operating in theta. However, theta hypnosis downloads the parent's statement as a "fact" about self, a limiting "programmed" belief in the child's subconscious mind.

Unedited subconscious recordings, programmed as literal truths, are used by the mind to shape our behavior, which in turn, determines our future life experiences. The consequences of negative "coaching" are revealed in workshops I've attended when people muscle test for the belief statement "I love myself." From 80 to 90% of the participants do not test positive for that belief. This conclusion is disastrous! If you do not love yourself, your subconscious behavior will sabotage your life's wishes to justify that negative belief. By definition, if a person does not love themselves, they will not find true love because they cannot accept someone's love if they believe themselves unlovable.

The negative perceptions of "self" unconsciously acquired in our youth invisibly sabotage the wishes and desires we hold in our conscious mind. When the conscious mind desires to improve our lot in life, the negative programs in the subconscious are filling our thoughts with deprecating self-talk 95% of the day. This "noise" in our heads emphasizes our inabilities, our weaknesses, our failures, and offers up any excuse that will cause us to give up on our wishes.

While the awareness of "self" just offered is self-empowering, book knowledge alone will not change your life. To move forward requires action. We must stop listening to the disempowering subconscious mind chatter, put our hands on the wheel, and heed the wishes of our best GPS system, our conscious mind.

Awakening to the knowledge of being programmed is transformative. No matter how low you might be in your life at this moment, owning the fact you are running on old programs and then taking the personal responsibility to put your hands on the wheel and rewrite those disempowering programs is the first step in self-empowerment and transforming your life.

While this sounds like pie-in-the-sky wishfulness in this time of global crises, more and more people are awakening to their innate powers every day. Especially powerful stories of transformation come from the lives of those referred to as resilient wonders. These are individuals that come from the worst possible childhood environments and pull themselves up by their own bootstraps to become leaders in our civilization.

One such resilient wonder is my friend Kirk Nugent. Kirk's life story makes Charles Dickens' novels read like Dr. Seuss. Most people whose developmental childhood experiences resembled Kirk's are either dead or in prison.

In a manner similar to taking the "red pill" in the Matrix movies, Kirk awoke from the horrors of his developmental programming. He began to train his consciousness to stay mindful, to stop defaulting to the defeatism of his limiting subconscious programs. Kirk's recounting of his story reveals that the trip up the ladder is not always easy. When letting go of his guard, Kirk's subconscious mind would unconsciously sabotage his conscious mind's efforts to shake his grossly dysfunctional developmental programs.

In Depression to Destiny, Kirk offers readers valuable lessons in learning to overcome the fear and the defeatism of our developmental programming. Kirk's engaging story provides a life-changing compilation of personal experiences that reveal how our thoughts, emotions, and actions shape every aspect of our perceived reality. Kirk's life lessons on his journey offer earned wisdom to enhance the quest and mission for a life well-lived.

For many seekers, a "life coach" is often necessary to instill enthusiasm and direction to energize us to get us off our duffs and encourage us to move toward our "Happily Ever After" goal. Toward manifesting that end, I highly recommend Kirk's informative book, for it offers readers an opportunity to move beyond misperceived limitations and write new empowering stories for themselves, their children, and the world.

Bruce H. Lipton, Ph.D., Stem cell biologist and bestselling author of The Biology of Belief, Spontaneous Evolution and The Honeymoon Effect

CONTENTS

CHAPTER 1
DEAD ON ARRIVAL 14

CHAPTER 2
THE RESPONSIBILITY OF CHOICE 36

CHAPTER 3
THE POWER OF CHOICE 58

CHAPTER 4
CHOOSING TO LIVE 74

CHAPTER 5
PURSUE YOUR PASSION 94

CHAPTER 6
THE COURAGE TO PERSIST 118

CHAPTER 7
THE BEAUTY OF MONEY 142

CHAPTER 8
THE ANSWER IS ALWAYS LOVE 156

CHAPTER 9
WHEREVER YOU GO, THERE YOU ARE 170

INTRODUCTION

"The works that I do shall ye do also, and greater works than these shall ye do."

Jesus the Christ

By the age of seventeen, my self-esteem was utterly shattered, and my dreams were dead in the water. However, I listened to a motivational speaker, and he spoke life back into my dreams. As I kept listening to his words, the dry bones began to shake and rattle. My once dead dreams and ideals began to take on a new form, new flesh, and new skin. And as he prophesied into my life, behold I was resurrected a new man.

From Depression to Destiny is my gift to you, my way of paying it forward. I've seen too many souls living in regret, upset that it is almost sunset, and yet they own no assets, be it physical or spiritual. Souls who have lost their way. Souls who've endured so much that they've stopped yearning, stopped striving to manifest their greatness. Instead, they operate every day in 'survival mode' just trying to make it through the day.

Life was meant to be enjoyed, not endured. You are Heaven's most magnificent creation, and within you lies a god, a god who has somehow forgotten that they are a god. Jesus was very aware of this when he asked, "Don't you know that ye are gods, and all of you are children of the Most High?"

The purpose of this book is to wake that God up, to place your 'Higher-Self' in the driver's seat, and have that consciousness navigate your life through chaos and conflict into the land of milk and honey. All that is required is your faith and your willingness to open your mind to ideas that might appear to be outside of our conventional programming. If thou canst believe, all things are possible to him that believes. The days and nights of you wandering in the wilderness are over. It is time to renew your mind and enter into your promised land. It is time to claim that which is rightfully yours, that which was given to you from the Divine. It is time to start fully experiencing the deliciousness and bounty of life.

So the question is, "Can these bones live?" Without a shadow of a doubt, the answer to that question is "Affirmative." You were born to win and destined to be great. Magnificence was chiseled into your heart, when God made you, He was showing off. The power to change your life lies in the ability to change your mind. I know that sounds unbelievably simple, and it is. If you are open to looking at your life from a 'higher' perspective, by the time you've read the last page of this book, you will be fully equipped to take your life in whatever direction that you find most pleasing to you. Enjoy the journey; I bid you bliss.

Given with much Love and from my heart to yours.

Kirk Nugent

Light Worker, Systems Buster, Illusion Crusher.

CHAPTER 1

DEAD ON ARRIVAL

> "I see dead people."
> "Where do you see them?"
> "Everywhere!"
> *The Sixth Sense*

Dead (adj): Lifeless, unresponsive or inactive, exhausted, deceased, defunct, perished.

According to the Social Security Administration, of those Americans who reach the age of sixty-five, "45 percent are dependent on relatives, 30 percent must live on charity, 23 percent are still working, and only 2 percent are self-sustaining."

Imagine that! After toiling for almost five decades at a job, most Americans could not pick success out of a police lineup. They are clueless as to what success looks like. They are not familiar with her scent, her mannerisms, her language, or her identity. This book however, is not just about financial prosperity, though that is a part of it. This book was written with the sole purpose of giving you the blueprint to a more gratified and fulfilled life. Your life was meant to be lived on your terms, whatever those terms are. If it were not, you would not have been given free-will.

Choice is what separates us from the animals. A bird cannot decide that it is not going to fly south for the winter, nor can a salmon choose not to swim upstream to mate. When was the last time you heard a rooster saying, "I'm just not in the mood to crow this morning, I think I'm going to just rest my vocal cords for a while and whisper sweet nothings in the ear of these hens whenever they decide to wake up."

How about a lion, lying on the plains of Africa contemplating its future, "After giving this idea some intense thought, I think I will refrain from the hunt for the next thirty days. Maybe I'll do an extended spiritual fast and finish that up with a green smoothie, and a juice cleanse. Yes, that will definitely accelerate my ascension process."

Animals have no choice in the matter. Their lives are presided over by instinct. They are slaves to their instinct, as we are slaves to our habits. Your job is to become a master of choice. Before we can break out of a prison cell, we must first realize that we're locked up. So let's take a quick snapshot of where the typical American finds himself on the success ladder. I'm sure the outlook is not much better for the rest of the world.

The Surgeon General has declared obesity to be an epidemic in America. He said that this could quite possibly be the first generation that will not outlive their parents. We are digging our graves with our teeth. Heart disease and cancer are two major killers in this country. People are dying from stress-related causes every day. The average American suffers their first major heart attack on Monday morning between the hours of 7 and 9 AM. In other words, Americans are dying to go to work.

Now, if you combine the statistics from the Social Security Administration and the statement from the Surgeon General, you'll find that by the age of sixty-five, most Americans are dead, dying, or dead broke. Why is that? Why do fifty percent of all marriages end in divorce? According to Men's Health magazine, an unhappy marriage increases your chance of getting sick by thirty-five percent and shortens your life by four years. Women who are not in a nurturing relationship have a higher rate of breast cancer, and men who are unhappy with their jobs have a higher rate of heart disease. If you can't find a way to live in peace (with yourself), chances are you will soon be resting in it. So why do we go about finding these updated and upgraded ways to sabotage our success and well-being?

We are shipping jobs overseas in unprecedented numbers. There was a time when it was said that if you're not fired in enthusiasm, chances are you will be fired, with enthusiasm! Nowadays, it doesn't matter if you're as enthused as Richard Simmons after an early morning jog and a banana, pineapple, orange, and mango smoothie. No one is immune to being outsourced, downsized, or just plain terminated. I've heard it whispered in corporate corners that in the next four years, the most difficult full-time job in America will be trying to find one. If you're under thirty-five, you stand a better chance of seeing a UFO landing on the White House lawn and aliens exiting the vehicle, while doing the James Brown dance, than seeing a social security check. We work just hard enough to keep from getting fired, and they pay us just enough to keep us from quitting. Due to a lack of passion for their current vocation, most Americans stop looking for work once they've found a job. I asked a young lady the other day, "How long have you been working here?" She said, "Ever since they threatened to fire me."

The state of Massachusetts did a research experiment, and they attempted to figure out why it is that some people under the age of fifty died from their first major heart attack while others survived. They found that the number one reason why people under fifty didn't survive their first major heart attack had nothing to do with cholesterol or genetic predisposition. The main reason these people died was that they suffered from a lack of job satisfaction. Why is it that the typical

American has a job that is held but hated? We're in relationships that are tolerated. Our dreams have either deteriorated or evaporated, or we've sat on them so long that they might as well be confiscated. The average American that is holding down a nine to five is agitated and aggravated. Their stomachs are ulcerated. We've become a nation of passionless people; basically, we are the living dead, walking around waiting to be boxed and buried.

According to the Suicide and Crisis center's website, an average of one person every eighteen minutes dies by suicide. They went on to state that suicide is the eleventh leading cause of death in America, compared to homicide, which is the fourteenth. So basically, more people kill themselves than kill each other. We are stunned when we learn that some of our most 'successful' idols succumb to suicide. Kurt Cobain, Donny Hathaway, Phyllis Hyman, Dana Plato, Whitney Houston, and Vincent van Gogh are just a few of the exceptionally gifted among us who, for whatever reason, simply got tired of living. Even though most of us might not have consciously contemplated suicide, we lead self-destructive lives by the company that we keep, the damaging relationships that we engage in, the food that we put in our bodies, and the garbage that we allow to enter our minds. Let's face it; we are not leading fulfilling lives. We're on a collision course with cancer and heart disease is just a heartbeat away.

The conventional American family is living paycheck to paycheck, and statistics indicate that, that family is only two paychecks away from being homeless. Furthermore, the SUV that they're driving is only one paycheck away from being repossessed.

In the book, 'The Two-Income Trap' by Elizabeth Warren and Amelia Warren Tyagi, it is stated that having a child is the single best predictor that a woman will end up in financial ruins. Home foreclosures have more than tripled in less than twenty-five years.

Americans are very familiar with the first rule of personal finance, which states that bills travel through the mail at twice the speed of checks. We know that the leading cause of divorce in this country is from arguments concerning money, not adultery. Seventy percent of incarcerated felons are imprisoned because they engaged in some inappropriate means to acquire wealth. Make no mistake about it; the average American is stressed and feeling out of control. Ironically, we feel good about ourselves to the exact degree that we feel we're in control of our own lives. So how do we gain more control over our lives to feel better? After all, when we feel better, we tend to live longer, healthier, happier lives.

In a futile attempt to escape the pain of our wretched reality, we tend to turn to 'Reality TV.' The average American watches over twenty-nine hours of television per week. Yet no one needs to be told that you do not become a millionaire by watching, 'Who wants to be a Millionaire?' That's just not how it works in the real world. We instinctively know that this is no time to be young and restless, searching for blind dates and shipmates. This is the time to be bold and beautiful, yet we seldom act on that idea. We rarely follow our guiding light; instead, we sit comatose in our comfort zone, allowing fear to be a factor. Sure, there are lovely programs on television, and a selective approach is always advisable, but most families leave the television on all day. They are mesmerized by it, and when we begin to consider how that time could efficiently be invested to move us closer towards our true desires, we start to realize that we've developed a tendency to major in minor things. We've been doing things wrong for so long that they've become traditionally right. Not only have we become volunteer victims, but now we are actively cosigning in our demise.

Over 26.5 million prescriptions were written over a 12 month period for Ambien, a sleep aid. The question that puzzles me is this: why is it that after an exhausting day at work, being stuck in rush hour traffic not once but twice, dropping off and picking up kids from daycare, preparing dinner, and helping kids with homework, so many people are having difficulties sleeping? One would naturally expect the average American to be exhausted after such a grueling schedule.

I use the term, 'average American' a lot, when ironically no one when asked in the third grade, 'What do you want to be when you grow up?" answers, "I know, I know, I want to be AVERAGE! Yeah, that sounds really good, I WANT TO BE AVERAGE!"

No one says, by age sixty-five, I want to be struggling! I want to be up to my nose in debt, and I want my health to be in constant decline. I want a credit score somewhere around room temperature. Yup, when I grow up, I want to be in an unloving relationship, divorced at least three times. Oh yea, and I definitely want my children to resent me. Yup, that's what I'm striving for. That's why I'm working so hard to get all these A's because I intend to be average. I want to experience foreclosures and repossessions, golly gosh, that has such a nice ring to it." No one ever says that, yet this is where ninety-five percent of us end up. Why is that?

The last thing any child wants to be is average. They subconsciously understand that average is the best of the worst, the worst of the best, the top of the bottom, the bottom of the top. In other words, there is no greatness in being average, and children instinctively know that they were born to win, destined to be great.

That's why they dream big dreams and have high ideals. Children are natural visionaries.

So what happened between the cradle and the grave? Between the invincible child in the third grade and the deteriorated older adult in the rocking chair, living in regret? Where did all that greatness go? How did that old man end up there, when he was once that little boy in the third grade saying, "One day I'm going to rule the world?" Was the child so ignorant that all he dreamt were impossible dreams, or was the man so conditioned, that he eventually made the possible, impossible? To answer that, we have to go back and examine the child and then the man.

When a child comes into this world, he/she comes in as pure potential. Let's assume that the child is a boy (it will save me the trouble of saying he or she throughout this example). The child is born with only two fears; the fear of falling and the fear of loud noises. In other words, he was not born with the fear of, "I wonder what the neighbors will think if I decided to pursue my passion?" He was not born with the fear of other people's opinions. He instinctively lived above the good opinions of others. Later in life, he will be taught to consider how the neighbors might react to his actions because, in this superficial world of ours, image is everything, and it is better to fit in rather than to stand out.

Have you ever observed a baby crying, and then immediately, the parent does something that the child thought was funny, so he starts laughing hysterically? I've seen babies laughing with the stain of dried tears on their cheeks. This is conclusive evidence that a child lives in the moment. He is not concerned with the fact that a minute ago, he was upset. As far as the child is concerned, that is over and done. He doesn't hang on to past hurts; no, he lets go and lets God. Children can go from pissed to bliss in less than a second. Their sole concern is right now, this moment. Somehow a child understands that all he has is the present moment, and it is a gift, not promised to anyone.

So the child relishes the moment thoroughly. He's not concerned that in two hours he's going to be hungry and that beloved nipple is nowhere to be found. Place him in a car and take him for a ride during rush hour, while you're cursing the traffic, he's in awe of the vehicles. He instinctively sees beauty everywhere. As he grows older, the parents must become more vigilant because the child will jump from the top of the stairs. He will run out into traffic; he will touch a hot stove. This kid believes that he is indestructible. It is as though this child feels that he is God. Or on some deeper level, he understands that there is no separation between him and God. He understands that he is divine, and he is awestruck by all the divinity around him. He knows that he has an indestructible core, so he is absolutely fearless, and this fearlessness is characterized by two words: I CAN! As far as that child is concerned, nothing is impossible, and he can do it all.

Children are spontaneous, absolutely void of inhibitions. How many times have you observed an infant in his mother's arms and just out of curiosity, stuck his fingers in the mother's mouth while she was speaking? Perhaps he reached out and grabbed her hair, or snatched a cat by its tail? Children don't have a need to contemplate how they will appear in the eyes of others. As far as they are concerned, someone else's opinion of them is none of their business. That spontaneity is characterized by the words: I DON'T HAVE TO.

I don't have to do anything I don't feel like doing. I don't have to live to please others. I just have to be true to myself at all times. If I don't like this food, I'm not going to eat it in the hopes of not offending the chef. If I'm feeling a tad exhausted, I'm going to take a nap. For the child, life is nothing but a series of choices, and they always choose what brings them joy. It is that simple.

Children are made out of love; they are not concerned with your race, your gender, nationality, religious or sexual preferences. The only two things children are concerned with is giving and receiving love. A child has to be taught to hate because when they initially entered the planet, such as concept was alien to their consciousness. No child has ever entered our world with the idea that he should waterboard another human being, or murder someone because he disagrees with their religious practice.

It is the parent's job to bring that child back to 'reality.' To mold him and get him prepared for the ills and dangers of life. So they systematically set about restraining and confining the 'god' in him. To keep him safe, they consistently tell him, "No!", "Stop that!" "Don't touch that!" "Be quiet!" and "Why can't you be more like your sister?" But the child doesn't 'hear' those words.

Whenever the parent yells, "Stop, don't touch that! Get away from there! No!" what the child understands is that every time he tries to have a new experience, mommy and daddy get mad. Therefore new experiences must be bad.

"Be quiet!" The child interprets this to mean, "What I have to say doesn't matter."

"Why can't you be more like your sister?" In other words, I'm not good enough.

Some parents even go as far as saying that children should be seen and not heard; the ultimate validation of that child's irrelevance. A child ultimately remembers not what his parents did for him, but how those parents made him feel. It is those feelings that eventually shape his destiny.

After these messages are massaged into the child's brain day in and day out, the once fearless child now begins to develop inhibitions. He doesn't want mommy or daddy to be mad. The trauma of losing their love is far more than he could bear. The most dreadful thought for any child is that of "My mommy and daddy don't love me." As human beings, we have an inherent desire to move away from pain and towards pleasure. We will do more to avoid pain than we will ever do to gain pleasure. So being fearful of losing his parent's love, the child begins to lose his curiosity and take on more conforming behaviors. He begins to care what his peers think, so he 'acts' accordingly. After a few years, he's no longer an individual, just a drone in the system going along with the programming.

On his way to school, his parent's parting words are, "Be careful," which gets interpreted as, "Don't take any risk today. Be sure to stay in your comfort zone today." So the child is reared in a world where he is told more about his limitations than his potential. By default, he invests more emotionally in his limitations rather than his potential.

He is subconsciously programmed to seek security rather than opportunity. He is told to go to school and be sure to color within the lines. Strive for good grades, complete college, and get a good job. Keep your nose clean, and you've got it made. He is never taught anything about pursuing the desires of his heart. No, that is reserved for the fortunate few. He is never taught that his wealth lies in his ability to serve his fellow human being. He is taught how to figure out the square root of pi, but no one ever taught him how to figure out how long it will take his money to double at a fixed interest rate. He can tell you exactly where two trains will intersect if one left NY traveling at sixty miles per hour and another left Boston traveling at eighty-five miles per hour. What he cannot tell you is how to deal with difficult people, how to manage stressful situations, how to lead with love, or how to show up with compassion and empathy. He was never taught that his success in life is directly related to his ability to manage all of his relationships, especially the relationship he has with himself.

By the time he's ready for college, he has been successfully programmed to self-destruct. He's been trained in one of two ideologies or a combination of both. This child has been successfully programmed on how to be a good employee. In other words, he has been programmed to go out into the world and create more wealth for wealthy folks (the so-called Elite) while he struggles to get by. If not a good employee, then an excellent patriotic soldier is the next obvious option. Again, he's sold on the idea of giving his life to protect the interest of the wealthy. In the process of accomplishing these goals, he's also sold on the idea that he is not good enough, and therefore he needs to CONSUME, CONSUME, CONSUME. As you and I both know, consumption is good for the ego and even better for the economy.

He's now a full-fledged consumer who seeks his identity in the brand names that he places himself in debt to purchase. His heart is put on the back burner because now, it's all about the image. He needs to carve out his own identity; he needs to be different; he needs to rebel. So he does this by looking and acting exactly like everyone in his peer group.

When it is time to choose a major and decide upon a career path, his heart is telling him that he would find unspeakable bliss in putting on a size 22 shoe, a red rubber nose, orange hair, paint his face and just be a clown, entertaining and bringing joy to children for the rest of his life. A decision that would have been so obvious at age two is now ludicrous to the alleged intellectually superior man. Be a clown? What are you, nuts? Where's the money in that? Where's the job security? My parents would kill me for wasting their money on college tuition. My dad is a doctor, and if I don't become a doctor, I'll get kicked out of the family's will. I'm going to med school.

So he's off to med school, which brings him absolutely no joy. He struggles to stay awake in the boring anatomy lectures. His only delight is his devoted girlfriend. She assists him in his studies after class. She is by far the most caring person that he's ever met. In his eyes, she's beyond gorgeous. Her beauty is illogical, irrational, unreasoned, and unwarranted. She has no business being so attractive. She is visually arresting and fiercely feminine; he is intrigued by her intellect and fascinated with her features. It's evident that when God created her, the 'Do Not Disturb' sign was hung on the door, and The Good Lord worked through lunch on this particular project. This young man's heart is whispering, 'This is the woman for you. You are soul mates connected from the eve of a previous life.' But once again, a decision that would have been crystal clear at age two is far too complicated at twenty. He knows that he cannot bring this woman back to his home. She's Palestinian, and he's Jewish. He's black; she's white. He's catholic; she's protestant. He's middle class, and she's lower class. I don't care, pick your stereotype, and let's move on with the analogy.

According to a study done by Cornell University, there is nothing unique about this story. They interviewed several thousand senior citizens and asked them, "What was it that they regretted the most in their lives?" Without exception, they all stated that the thing that cost them the most pain was nothing that they did, but rather the things that they failed to do, the passions that they failed to pursue.

He subconsciously knows that this relationship is not going to last, so he finds new and improved ways to sabotage and destroy it. He struggles through med school, barely making passing grades, and now he's off to a career that he abhors. He finds being around sick people all day to be very depressing. His career brings him far more pain than pleasure.

On the dating scene, he's met a few interesting people, but none that moved him like his girlfriend in college. None that made his heart sing and placed his mind in a perpetual state of nirvana like his previous girlfriend did. Eventually, he settles for the next best thing, gets married, and has the suggested 1.2 kids, the house with the white picket fence on top of the hill. To the untrained eye, he and his wife are the epitomai of success, but look a little deeper, scratch below the surface, and you'll find a couple that is dying together rather than living together. His is a life that's void of bliss, yet he continues to make decisions based on how he believes he will be perceived. There's very little passion between him and his wife, and somehow he has the gut feeling that the postman has been ringing twice.

It doesn't matter how this story ends. What matters is that when a man is deeply asleep, nature sends pain and suffering to awake him. I assure you that this typical story is not your destiny. The very fact that you have this book in your hands is indicative of your desire for something more. You're beginning to question the Matrix that had you asleep.

To rise and claim your glorious destiny is simple, not necessarily easy, but simple. If you want to be something different in life, you must begin by doing something different. Remember that a good definition of insanity is to keep on doing the same things over and over, expecting different results. Lao Tzu once said that if you do not change direction, you may end up where you are heading.

I've heard it said that the reason they call it 'The American Dream' is because you have to be asleep to believe that garbage. That is not necessarily true; your dreams are available to you. They are there for you to achieve, but first, you must believe that they are possible. You must believe that they are within reach. Whenever I step back and observe the greatness, the miracle, the divinity of the human mind, I'm in awe of how many are living in lack and despair. It is as though we are like fish swimming in a vast ocean crying out to God, pleading, "Dear God if only I had some water!"

Belief is the first key to resurrecting these dead dreams. After all, it was our belief system that buried us in the first place. One of the greatest teachers of all times taught us that if we can just believe, all things are possible to the man that does. Our beliefs are nothing more than stories and ideas that we have repeated to ourselves thousands of times. To change our beliefs, we simply have to change the story that we are telling ourselves daily. In the old paradigm that we were living, the idea that we were sold and most of us bought into was, "When I see it, I will believe it." With the new energy and consciousness that is now bombarding the planet, the new paradigm is: When you believe it, you will see it.

In the following pages, I am going to lay out some simple steps that will get you from where you are to where you want to be. Everything is a process; all you have to do is learn how to become a master of methods.

PURSUE YOUR PASSION

This is your life,

Your purpose on this Earth is not to please me.

Nor is it to fulfill your parent's unrealized dreams.

You were not placed here to make concessions so that they could be proud,

So they could brag about their seed,

Fulfill some unfulfilled childhood emotional needs.

Let them be proud of their very own deeds

This is your life!

I came to shine light into the dark

And like a dog against a hydrant, I am leaving my mark!

We were not sent here to invest in someone

Else's idea of what we should be

The complacent life does not stimulate me.

So forgive me if I feel no compassion

For those poor souls who live to follow the fashion.

Because if you want to live a life that's neither limited nor ration,

Then by God, you must pursue your passion.

They will tell you that it can't be done

As though you were delivered unto this world for your song to go unsung.

Let the world scream that unattainable theme

But for you, there is no such thing as an impossible dream.

Ain't no mystery, check the history.

Look at the life of Oprah Winfrey,

Muhammad Ali, Mahatma Gandhi.

Remember what they told Walt Disney?

They said, "Young man you must be blind

You must have lost your rodent loving mind!

Because no one would ever pay to be entertained by a mouse

Or anything of that kind."

Now Disney is worth more than everyone in this room combined.

Pursue your passion!

Steven Spielberg was kicked out of the University of Southern California

Film School because his grades weren't good enough.

Pursue your passion!

Russell Simmons refused to sign Madonna

Because he thought she had no talent.

Pursue your passion!

Brandy's teacher told her she was too ugly to be an actress.

Pursue your passion!

Bill Cosby used to shine shoes in front of Temple University.

Pursue your passion!

Michael Jordan was benched on his basketball team in High school

Pursue your passion!

Larry Bird was benched his entire freshman year of college.

Pursue your passion!

Here is proof that greatness is born out of zero doubt

In 1962 Decca Records dismissed four young musicians

Told them that groups with guitars were on their way out.

They left without a contract

But refused to walk on pins and needles

Months later they released their first album

And called themselves, "The Beatles."

Pursue your passion!

Colonel Sanders was 65 when he fried his first piece of chicken,

Made millions after he convinced us that it was finger-lickin.'

Pursue your passion!

Lauren Hill was booed at the Apollo

Pursue your passion!

Luther Vandross lost at the Apollo

Not once, not twice, but three times.

You've got to keep coming back, ladies and gentlemen.

Forget the limitations set by your fellow man,

Because when you pursue your passion,

Provisions will be provided for your plan.

Let others lead small lives, but not you.

Let others be imprisoned by their fears, but not you.

Let others use their race, their gender,

Their sexual orientation as a crutch, but not you.

Let others be concerned about what the neighbors

Might think, say or do, but this is not for you.

Leave that to the politicians, the governors,

Start caring about other people's opinion

And you'll become their prisoner.

So now that you know that impossible is a word

Found in the dictionary of fools,

What are you going to do?

What are you going to do with the rest of your life?

What two things do you want

To be said about you when you die?

I never listened to what the pessimists are telling me

Because I know that the wealthiest place

On the planet is the cemetery.

There you will find books that were never written,

Loved ones that were never forgiven,

Ideas that were smitten

And dreams that were forbidden.

Soil that was never tilled,

Cathedrals that were never built.

Restaurants that were never opened

Chefs that never knew they were smoking.

Paintings that were never drawn nor hung,

Songs that were neither composed nor sung

Souls that never acted on what they really wanted to do

So don't you dare die with your greatness buried within you.

It's all an illusion, don't you invest in their lies

Their forecast of economic woes and financial demise.

My God has an infinite supply, so no need to lie when I testify

That regardless of the economy, you cannot be denied.

It matters not if they raise the terrorist threat level

To hot pink, burgundy or fuchsia

You were born to control your future.

Don't let 'em fool you.

You were born to win, destined to be great

Magnificence was chiseled into your heart,

When God made you, he was just showing off.

Discover your divine assignment, and you'll have no reason to retreat

Discover your passion, and you'll laugh in the face of defeat.

Indifferent to the pressures felt, and you do not buckle like a belt.

Declare today that you refuse to lose

Because you can either live your dreams,

Or you can live your excuse.

So even when I'm old and grey,

I'll still be commanding the stage,

My words will still be smoking off the page.

So understand, this ain't no phase,

Because every day I learn a new lesson,

My best poem has yet to be written

And I'm not leaving until what I came to give has been given.

I'll be 99 on the mic, and I'll still be spittin'

Still be rippin'

Still be giving

Still be driven

So let my tombstone read:

Here lies Kirk and he died LIVING.

Pursue your passion!

*The complete version of the Pursue Your Passion poem can be found in my book, Answer The Call.

CHAPTER 2

THE RESPONSIBILITY OF CHOICE

> "It is in the moment of decision
> that our destiny is decided."
> *Anthony Robbins*

DISEMPOWERMENT

Shelley Parris, a friend of mine, once wrote, "Most people aren't aware of the shackles firmly planted on their minds. They never realize that they are inmates, labeled "Property of the State," state of mind that is."

I believe that most of us either overlook this truth, or maybe we're just totally unaware of the fact that the mind, our mind, is the most powerful tool available to us on the planet.

As a child, we're taught to look outside of ourselves for all the answers. Mom knows best, or your teacher knows best. It is rude to question 'authority.' We are constantly bombarded with information from the 'experts.' In school, we're not tested on our ability to reason and solve problems. No, our system is one based on remembering facts and regurgitating historical events. We soon begin to doubt our inner radar, and we look everywhere but inside for all the answers that are already there.

Very soon, we begin to give our power and responsibility away. We quickly learn how to play the blame game and manipulate other people's emotions to serve our needs.

I cringe when I hear adults giving away their power by saying something as asinine as, "He made me mad!"

Really? And exactly how did he manage to accomplish this? Of course, they'll go on to explain with great emotional fervor what the offending party did. However, I fail to understand the correlation. Though I can recognize that he/she was using poor judgment, I can never get the individual to accurately state how someone else can make them mad. Typically, after several futile attempts to explain their situation, they usually get frustrated and then direct their anger towards me. They often respond with something like this:

Angry Person: "Now you're making me mad."

Kirk Nugent: "I see. Are you saying mad, as in angry?"

Angry Person: "Yea, mad, angry, upset, whatever you want to call it."

Kirk Nugent: "Aren't those emotions?"

Angry Person: "Of course they're emotions, what do you think they are, vegetables?"

Kirk Nugent: "Do you mind if I asked you a question?"

Angry Person: "You just did, want to try for two?"

Kirk Nugent: "Let's assume that there was a magic genie in a bottle, and he offered to give you ten million dollars and perfect health for the next eighty-five years, and all you had to do was remain in a state of bliss for the next five minutes."

Angry Person: "Uh-huh."

Kirk Nugent: "Then here comes James, and he did what he did, and said exactly what he said to you previously. Would you get mad at him?"

Angry Person: "And lose my ten mill? What are you nuts?"

Kirk Nugent: "Why not? He displayed the same lack of judgment that he did previously."

Angry Person: "Son, if I had ten million dollars, I wouldn't be thinking about James."

Kirk Nugent: "So you're saying that regardless of what he did, you would choose not to be mad?"

Angry Person: "No doubt."

Kirk Nugent: "So being mad is a choice? Is that what you're saying?"

Angry Person: "No, that's what you're saying. You're always coming at me with these semantics.

I'm just saying that for ten million dollars, I would let it slide."

Kirk Nugent: "You would choose to let it slide?"

Angry Person: "I guess... whatever."

Kirk Nugent: "Well, if that is true, then the converse must be true as well, don't you think?"

Angry Person: "What do you mean?"

Kirk Nugent: "You chose not to let it slide, and therefore James didn't make you mad.

You chose to be upset."

Angry Person: "You're beginning to piss me off. BYE!"

This lesson repeats until the lesson is learned. Blaming is the pastime of people who deny their responsibility, and unfortunately, most of us will go to our graves without fully comprehending this elementary, yet critical lesson. The concept of an emotional response being a choice is foreign to most, and such a thought is an outcast in the outer limits of their mind, an alien in their consciousness.

PERSPECTIVE:

One of the hallmarks of a highly evolved person is that they understand that life is about choices. We get to choose how we respond to everything that happens to us, and it is in these choices that our lives soar towards success or sink towards failure. The important thing in life is not what happens to us but how we choose to explain to ourselves what has happened and how we respond to what is happening. Those are the two critical factors that either enrage or enlighten us. So, choose not to be offended. Being offended is a weakness of the ego.

Imagine how empowered you would feel if instead of explaining your days at the office as good days and bad days, you told yourself that you were having a 'character building' and a 'character-revealing' day? How would you feel if you could keep in mind at all times that any day above ground is a good day?

About six o'clock one morning, I was checking out of my hotel, and I noticed a gentleman sitting in the lobby reading the comics in the newspaper. He appeared to be in his mid-seventies. As I fumbled with my luggage, I greeted him, "Good morning Sir. How are you today?"

He put the paper down for a minute and observed me from head to toe. He smiled effortlessly and said, "Young man, if I were doing any better, I would need a twin."

As I waited for my driver to take me to the airport, I inquired about his age. He was ninety-four. I was shocked. He could tell that I doubted his age, so he showed me his passport to prove the accuracy of his statement. I asked him, "What is the secret to your longevity?"

He answered my question by posing a question of his own. He asked, "Young man, how do you know if today is going to be a great day?"

I responded, "I don't know, I'm not clairvoyant. Some days you wake up, and you just feel great, I guess."

He said, "If you wake up, and there's not a chalk outline around your body, it's going to be a great day."

Point well taken; it's a great day because you're alive. It's a choice, but you have to decide on it. Because of that conversation, I no longer refer to my days as good or bad; I have character-building days and character-revealing days.

STRESS:

I once read a study that was conducted, and it stated that if you extracted blood from a human being when that person is in an extreme state of anger and then injected the blood into a pig, the pig would die from the high level of acid in the blood.

We know that high blood pressure and a host of other ailments evolve through stress, and if we could eliminate stress, we would eliminate all of these diseases. There have been countless studies conducted that prove that negative emotions such as fear, worry, and anger dramatically lowers our immune system. Ulcers are caused by excessive stomach acid, and studies of patients have shown that anger and hostility increase stomach acidity.

Psychological stress has also been shown to increase susceptibility to viral infection. Subjects exposed to stress showed increases in infection rates from 74% to 90%, and clinical colds rose from 27% to 47%. Earlier studies have shown that medical students have an increased risk of mononucleosis during examination periods (McEwen & Stellar, 1993). Yet stress is optional.

I believe that the first place to start when striving for a fulfilling life is with good health. That should be our number one goal. It is challenging to experience life as it was meant to be experienced if your health is always failing. Most people never consider their health until it starts to fail. They take immaculate care of their cars (which can always be replaced), but their bodies are kept dirty on the inside by the toxins that they feed it. Everything that includes the well-being of their body is done with very little attention and with great haste. Meals are rushed, the diet that the body is fed is by default and not by design. Even something as critically important as rest is usually interrupted by an alarm clock.

CHOICE:

I recall watching an interview between Barbara Walters and Christopher Reeve after he had been paralyzed for several years. She asked him if he was frustrated by the fact that he was once a very physical person, and now he's confined to a wheelchair. He replied, "It doesn't frustrate me that I'm physically paralyzed. It frustrates me to see people who are physically able, walking around paralyzed in the brain."

Remember the wisdom of Anthony Robbins, "It is in the moment of decision that our destiny is decided." It all boils down to the responsibility of choice.

Simple, but again not necessarily easy. How do you remain cool, calm, and collective when some inconsiderate soul comes along just to test your faith? How do you maintain composure in the face of incompetence? I'm not referring to biting your lips while your blood is boiling on the inside. No, that will do even more damage to your health. What I'm asking is, how do you get to a place of peace, where you're not even irritated by the irrational?

As within, so without:

Before we answer that, let me use an analogy that I heard from Dr. Wayne Dyer. When you squeeze an orange, what comes out? Most people will reply, juice, but I need you to be more specific. The correct answer would be orange juice. How about when you squeeze a grapefruit? The answer is obvious; grapefruit juice. Is it possible to squeeze an orange and get grapefruit juice? Of course not, the only thing you can get out of something was what was in it in the first place. So when someone comes along and makes you mad, all that happened was that life just squeezed you, and what was inside came pouring out. If it weren't in there in the first place, it would've never have come out. As within, so without!

Michael Richards, better known as Kramer from the television sitcom Seinfeld, was heckled by a group of African Americans during one of his stand-up comedy routines. Being offended, he retorted by calling them the 'N' word and reminding his hecklers that, "Fifty years ago we'd (meaning: including himself) have you hanging upside down with a fork up your ass."

He asked security to throw them out because they were niggers, and he went on to justify his statements by saying, "That's what happens when you interrupt a white man."

Now, think back to a time when you were angry. Has someone ever made you so angry that you thought to yourself, "Man, I would love to take a butcher knife and hack this fool to pieces, then cook him in a stew and have him for dinner?"

Chances are, such a thought has never entered your mind simply because it's not a part of your consciousness, yet that idea is not so far-fetched to Jeffrey Dahmer. Being a murderer and a cannibal, it is possible that those thoughts could find a place to fester and grow in his mind.

Had Michael Richards not held sacred in the outpost of his mind, the idea that African Americans are indeed niggers and should be lynched, there is absolutely no way such ideas would have entered his brain, much less left his mouth. All that happened was that he got squeezed by life (hecklers), and what was inside came out. Ironically, those were his exact words when he was on David Letterman's show explaining himself. He said, "It fires out of me…it comes through…the rage… it just comes out."

We all walk around with a mask (to a certain degree), and in times of emotional stress, life has a habit of removing the mask. How many times have you been in an argument with a friend or a loved one, and they end up saying some hurtful stuff that you had no idea they were thinking, or they brought up some event from the past that you thought was already behind you? Even when intoxicated, drunk words always stems from sober thoughts.

Most people, if asked to complete this statement, "Garbage in …" would answer, "Garbage out." Cute, but such a statement doesn't give the real picture. A more accurate statement would be "Garbage in. Garbage stays in. Garbage gets pregnant. Garbage has triplets and much more garbage out."

Human beings have a natural tendency to reflect their environment, so don't allow garbage in. Don't entertain your toxic friends that are always complaining and singing the, 'Somebody done me wrong' song. As long as you're not fed daily doses of garbage, it is less likely to be a part of you.

So getting back to being squeezed by life, one of the most effective ways to choose to be happy is to keep everything in perspective. If one year from today you can't recall what you were mad about last year on this date, then it wasn't worth you getting upset in the first place. Frankly, I can't think of anything worth driving your blood pressure through the roof.

There was a young girl who went away to college, and after some months she wrote to her parents. The letter read:

Dear Mom and Dad,

It has been three months since I left for college. I have been remiss in writing, and I am very sorry for my thoughtlessness in not having written before. I will bring you up to date now, but before you read on, please sit down. You are not to read any further unless you are sitting down, okay?

Well then, I am getting along pretty well now. The skull fracture and the concussion I got when I jumped out of the window of my dormitory when it caught fire shortly after my arrival are pretty well healed by now. I only spent two weeks in the hospital, and now I can see almost normally and only get those headaches once a day.

Fortunately, the fire in the dormitory and my jump were witnessed by an attendant at the gas station near the dorm, and he was the one who called the Fire Dept. and the ambulance. He also visited me at the hospital, and since I had nowhere to live because of the burnt out dormitory, he was kind enough to invite me to share his apartment with him. It's actually a basement room, but it's kind of cute. He is a wonderful boy, and we have fallen deeply in love and are planning to get married. We haven't set the exact date yet, but it will be before my pregnancy begins to show.

Yes, Mom and Dad, I am pregnant. I know how very much you are looking forward to being grandparents, and I know you will welcome the baby and give it the same love and devotion and tender care you gave me when I was a child. The reason for the delay in our marriage is that my boyfriend has some minor infection which prevents us from passing our premarital blood tests and I carelessly caught it from him. This will soon clear up with the penicillin injections I am now taking daily.

I know you will welcome him into the family with open arms. He is kind, and although not well educated, he is ambitious. Although he is of a different race and religion than ours, I know that your oft-expressed tolerance will not permit you to be bothered by the fact that his skin color is somewhat darker than ours. I am sure you will love him as I do. His family background is good too, for I am told his father is a vital gun runner in the village in Africa from which he comes.

Now that I have brought you up to date, I want to tell you there was no dormitory fire; I did not have a concussion or a skull fracture; I was not in the hospital; I am not pregnant; I am not engaged. I do not have syphilis, and there is no new boyfriend in my life. However, I am getting a D in sociology and an F in science; and I wanted you to see these grades in their proper perspective.

Your loving daughter,

Emily.

Shifting our perspective always brings us back to the realization that things are not as bad as we tell ourselves. Another cornerstone to having a positive, expectant outlook on life is an attitude of gratitude. Whenever I'm having a 'character building' day, I'll do something immediately to shift my energy to bring me back to a place of peace and thanksgiving. It could be something as simple as putting on a James Brown CD and blasting the track, "I Feel Good.' Try doing that while doing the James Brown dance, it is impossible to feel bad while doing that and singing at the top of your lungs, "I feeeeeel good."

Or I'll go on the internet and look at what's going on in other parts of the world such as Rwanda, Somalia, Iraq, or Afghanistan and be grateful that I'm not waking up to such horrid conditions.

Volunteer your time with disabled children or with seniors who are infirm and have no family. Being in a constant state of gratitude is one of the best ways to take control of your attitude, where the small irritants of life will become oblivious on the screen of your mental radar. Whenever some inconsiderate child of God cuts me off in traffic, I think to myself that he's probably late for work, and I'm grateful that I don't have a conventional nine to five.

If you intend to live your dreams and not your fears, then you must start by taking responsibility for every area of your life. Start by taking responsibility for your belief system, your thoughts, and your emotions. Understand that when you were born, you were blessed with free will, and therefore no one can make you do anything (assuming that you are an adult and not a child living under your parent's rule). People will try and manipulate you and use your fears against you, but fundamentally the choice lies with you.

Years ago, I was employed by a furniture store, and the regional manager felt a need to reprimand me. I was working in a store in New Jersey, and he needed me to drive to Pennsylvania to be formally chastised. I thought, "Pennsylvania? That's too far a distance to travel just to listen to his idiotic ranting". So I called him, "You're in New Jersey at least three times per week. May I meet you at one of the Jersey locations?"

His response, "Absolutely not, be in my office tomorrow by nine."

"In Pennsylvania? No, that's not going to happen."

"What did you say?"

"You heard me."

"Kirk, you'd better come to see me OR ELSE!"

"OR ELSE!" Wow! He's firing with big guns. "Or else? I guess he's trying to play on my fear of the unknown. He's anticipating that my mind is going to start racing with all these horror stories. What could be attached to the end of that, "Or else?"

Well, here's what I knew. He had the power to terminate me, nothing more. And since I've loved, laughed, prospered, and maintained my God-given sexiness for twenty-five years before I heard of this furniture chain. It would stand to reason that I will love, laugh, prosper, and continue to maintain my sexiness for another twenty-five years after my termination. Gifted with such impeccable logic, I felt compelled to inform this poor misguided soul, "Whatever or else is, you might as well move on to that, I'm NOT coming to see you."

He was rendered speechless by my response. Obviously, this is an intimidation tactic he'd effectively administered in the past. Why wasn't it working this time? He was accustomed to the other employees responding emotionally, out of the fear of losing their job. Reacting out of past conditioning, to be thankful that they had a job, after all, a lot of folks aren't that fortunate. I chose to respond logically. It just didn't make sense to me to drive six hours in traffic to see him, when he was scheduled to be fifteen minutes away from me the very next afternoon. If this was the price that I needed to pay to keep a job that no longer furnished my joy, then maybe this was Life's way of telling me that it's time to move on. I didn't believe that I would starve to death, nor would I lose my home. People are hired and fired consistently and live to tell about it. Why should my experience be any different? Besides, I am Kirk Nugent, and I do not buckle like a belt! (Did you catch that positive self-talk reinforcing the idea that I would be just fine?) You have to train the mind on how to respond calmly in what it has been programmed to perceive as a crisis.

Incidentally, that was my last job. Even though I wasn't terminated for my insubordination, I decided that this event was a sign from the Universe that I needed to quit spending forty hours per week building someone else's dream and get busy working on my own. I did. Leaving that job led to me pursuing my passion as a poet, becoming an inspirational speaker, author of several books, and the freedom to travel all across the globe. So looking back, a decision that would've enslaved most men, directly led to my emancipation. It all begins with choice.

Unfortunately, because of past programming, we tend to make choices that are fear-based and limiting instead of choices that will give us the life that we've dreamed of. Very seldom do we make choices beyond the scope of our belief. Somehow we find a way not to risk too much; therefore, we won't lose too much. We always seem to run back to our need to move away from what's painful towards that which is not painful.

So in short, we become imprisoned by our comfort zone. Breaking out of that comfort zone requires constant vigilance. Here is a simple exercise that will help you to be more aware of your thoughts.

Tomorrow upon arising, attempt to go through the day without judging anything, just be the observer. It is almost impossible to do because the mind is continually making judgments and evaluating every situation. What this exercise will do for you is force you to pay attention to your thoughts. You'll be aware of how many times you have a restricting thought regarding your abilities.

There is an adage that goes, "When I see it, I'll believe it," but if we understood the way that our mind works, we'd see that a more accurate statement would be, "When I believe it, I will see it."

The human brain processes 400 billion bits of information per second, but we're only aware of 2,000 bits. So how does the brain decide what to bring into our awareness and what to leave out? This job is left up to the Reticular Activating System (RAS).

Scientific research has established the fact that the RAS is a group of cells at the base of our brain stem (about the size of a little finger). It serves as a control center--sorting and evaluating incoming data. It's responsible for filtering out the important stuff from the unimportant so that you can function correctly. One of the ways in which the RAS figures out what is insignificant is based on the conversation that you have with yourself, in short, your belief system. The RAS, along with the subconscious mind, works to make your ideas and thoughts true. So it filters out of your awareness of anything that goes against your belief system. This is why it is so futile to attempt to change someone's religious or political beliefs. If a woman subconsciously believes that all men are dogs, immediately her RAS goes into action and screens out from her awareness the men that would not fit into the category of 'dogs.' Until she changes that belief system, all she sees, all she meets, and all she'll attract are 'dogs.'

Life will always meet us on our level of expectation, according to your faith, be it unto you. In the Bible, Job declares, "The thing that I've feared has come upon me." Whenever I give lectures, regardless of what country I am in, there's always someone in the audience that raises the issue that they don't wish to be broke, they don't want to be in an unloving relationship, but somehow, they are.

Let's go back to the analogy of the young lady complaining that ALL men are dogs. This woman might be wishing and hoping that all men are NOT dogs. She might be searching for a good man, but out of sheer frustration concludes that all men are INDEED dogs. The RAS is not concerned with her hopes and dreams; what it acts upon is her belief. Deep down, she believes that a man is going to jerk her around. Somewhere in her life, she accepted the program that men are only out for one thing, and they cannot be trusted. So even if a 'good' man manages to slip passed her sensors, she'll sabotage the relationship by saying, "This is too good to be true." or "This can't possibly be happening to me." and immediately the RAS goes to work to make her statements accurate. Whenever inner speech and desire are in conflict, inner speech always wins.

I've destroyed many relationships with women who loved me because I had a program running in my mind, which said that I wasn't worthy of being loved. Regardless of how much those women cared for me, it was impossible for those relationships to last because I had a filter that was screening out anyone who brought me anything that resembled love. It is incredible, the self-defeating thoughts that we have running through our minds at any given moment. That is why the exercise of going through the day without passing any judgment is critically important. If you cannot bring your thoughts under control, it is improbable that you will bring your life under control. A change in attitude is a change in position on Life's playing field.

I heard a television psychologist once say that if we keep experiencing the same results, regardless of how painful they are, there must be an emotional payoff. If there were no payoff, we would never repeat the process. I remember initially thinking that this guy is mentally unbalanced, if not demented. Where's the emotional payoff for a woman in an abusive relationship? I used to have the most painful Sickle Cell crisis as a child, and sometimes I would be admitted to the hospital for weeks at a time. Where was the payoff in that?

After paying closer attention to the underlying cause of the results that were showing up in my life and in the lives of others that I was intimately familiar with, I understood the truth in the psychologist's assessment. I started reflecting on my childhood and realized that I had a Sickle Cell crisis every year from age four until I was twelve. Between the ages of twelve and fifteen, I thrived in perfectly good health. Between the ages of fifteen and twenty, I had one crisis. So I began reflecting on what was going on in my life during those periods.

I came from a household where love was neither understood nor expressed. There was no proclamation of love or affection between my parents, and I always felt as though we (the children) were a mere financial burden to them. At age four, I was diagnosed with Sickle Cell Anemia, a blood disorder which among other things, can affect the circulation of oxygen throughout the body and causes excruciating pain in the joints. Based on the research available at the time when I was diagnosed, compounded by the fact that I was living in a third world country, the doctors predicted that I would be dead by the age of thirteen. Every three or four months, I would have these agonizing joint pains and a fever more persistent than the knock of a Jehovah's Witness. My eyes would turn bright yellow as my liver fought to remove the toxins from my blood. Needless to say, I've been at Death's door so many times that I could tell you what he was serving for dinner on any given Sunday. But according to the 'brain' on television, this was a choice. In all of this suffering, somehow, there was an emotional payoff that served me.

Whenever I was sick, my mom was always there to nurse me back to health. She would sit by my bedside and wipe the beads of sweat from my forehead. This would be one of those rare occasions where I felt like someone cared about me. My dad, on the other hand, was quite indifferent. He went about his daily routine. If I was admitted to the hospital, he never came to visit, nor did he ever express any concern for my well-being. Although I was only four at the time, I concluded that my dad didn't care. So here's the payoff. Whenever I was sick, I felt my mom's love, so it made sense to be sick as much as possible.

Shortly after my twelfth birthday, my mom moved to America for three years in the hopes of getting a visa and sending for the rest of the family. In the three years that she was gone, between the ages of twelve and fifteen, I never so much as caught a common cold. I knew that my dad didn't care. No payoff. No need to be sick. Between the ages of fifteen and nineteen, I'm rebelling; certainly didn't need the love or approval of my parents, so again, no need to be sick. Between nineteen and twenty, I was working full time at a hospital between the hours of midnight and eight in the morning. I would leave work and rush off to school (I was a full-time college student). I had to be in class by nine. I stayed until around four and spent the next five or six hours in the library. After a few months of this routine, I had my first Sickle Cell Crisis in eight years. The payoff: I was exhausted, my body needed rest! So as you can see, there was indeed a 'payoff' for all of these recurring crises.

I challenge you to take an in-depth look at your life and see what you've been attracting to yourself. Be silent for a while, reflect on your thoughts, and you'll be able to hear what you've been speaking into your life. Nothing happens by chance, everything by choice. Forget for a moment what you want; what you've earned is staring you in the face.

I AM:

Our words and thoughts have an uncanny habit of manifesting; I believe this is what is meant by, "In the beginning was the Word and the Word was made flesh." There's always a thought that precedes the word. So in the beginning, we had a thought, and then we spoke that thought, and eventually, that thought became real. (flesh) There are no coincidences; this Universe is held together by perfect Law and order. If we're going to reclaim our lives, then we must start at the beginning. We must begin by controlling our words and thoughts. Never allow a statement to leave your mouth that you don't want to see manifest in the 'real' world. If we truly understood the power of the spoken word, it would be evident that we cannot afford the luxury of a negative thought.

Question everything; nothing is so sacred that it cannot be questioned. Make sure that your beliefs empower and not imprison you. I know of a very devout Christian woman, she's now in her eighties and one of the most beautiful souls one could ever hope to meet on this sojourn. We were conversing, and she shared with me something that has been troubling her for the past fifty years. She assured me that she had served and worshiped God all of her life, but sometimes she just doesn't understand Him. She doesn't know why she has to struggle to make ends meet. She has kept the Commandments, she has given more than ten percent in her tithes and offerings, yet she hasn't prospered financially. She wanted to know why God has dealt with her in such a manner.

I assured her that she was not cursed, at least not by God. I told her that I'd heard her prayers, and they all sound pretty much like this. "Lord, I am not worthy; I am like a piece of filthy rag in thy holy sight. Lord, I am nothing, have mercy upon a poor soul." I told her that it is her own words that have been made flesh and are responsible for her financial affairs. State of affairs is always caused by the state of mind. If you go around claiming that you are not worthy, then the RAS goes right to work and makes sure those conditions manifest in your life. According to your faith, be it unto you. As a man thinketh in his heart, so is he. I instructed her to make the shift mentally, declare herself to be worthy. It may not seem like much, but it is a small shift with tremendous implications.

Muhammad Ali understood the power of the spoken word, as he was a master of the power of suggestion. He would predict the round that he would knock his opponent out, and his words would come to pass. All he did was plant the seed of doubt in his opponent's mind, and they would self-destruct in the predicted round. Ali knew that the two most powerful words in the Universe are: I AM. Whatever you attach to those words, you become. He never said, "Someday, I will be the greatest." His words were, "I AM the greatest!" He was repeating those words thousands of times per day before he even stepped into the ring. His RAS responded by affirming, "Indeed you are."

We must become that which we say we are. At the tomb of Lazarus, Jesus didn't say, "You know, I just might have the ability to resurrect." He declared with total confidence, "I AM the resurrection and the life." We are not what we think we are, but what we think, we are! Or as Earl Nightingale states, "We become what we think about."

How many times do we go around affirming, "I am broke, I can't afford that, I'm no good at math, I am not a people's person." We've planted the seed for our demise, and at the time of harvest, we ask, "How could this happen to me?" Simply, by our words, we're justified; by our words, we are condemned. Whatever you think about expands; therefore, develop the habit of focusing on what you want, not on what you don't want. Words can create or destroy, enrich, or diminish. In the book of Proverbs, we are reminded that death and life are in the power of the tongue. Words are the currency of this marketplace called Life, so invest them wisely.

So how do we resurrect the dreams that have been dead and buried in the recesses of our minds? Start by taking TOTAL responsibility for every area of your life. Know that you're responsible for your emotions. Consider emotions to be like a gun that's in your hand, even if you allow someone else to pull your trigger. It was your gun, in your hand, so you pay the price. Never allow anyone to fool you with your emotional trigger. Practice the art of non-judgment so that you can be aware of your thoughts. Never dwell on an idea that you don't want to see manifested in your world. As I said, the formula is simple, not necessarily easy (at first). It will take discipline, tons of discipline to master your mind, but once you do that, you become unstoppable. Master your mind and you will master your world. You were born to win, destined to be great. So never confuse bad management of your thoughts with destiny.

"Everybody sooner or later sits down to a banquet of consequences. Ironically we spend a lifetime preparing the menu but are often dissatisfied when the meal is finally served."

- Robert Louis Stevenson

In one of my previous books, 'The Unpopular Truth' I declared that:

I believe in a lot of things

But most of all, I believe in the power within.

I believe in poetry, persistence, and passion,

I believe in chasing impossible dreams

Because fear always buckles in the presence of action.

I believe that we're the cause of our unhappiness

I believe that there is so much inside of us that we haven't tapped as yet.

I believe in experiencing life through every single breath

I believe that there's greatness in each and every one of you

And I challenge you not to settle for anything less.

That challenge still stands, and I intend to see you at the top.

CHAPTER 3

THE POWER OF CHOICE

"To truly grow you have to be willing at any moment
To sacrifice what you are for what you can become."
Ralph Waldo Emerson

As you continue to monitor your thoughts, start deciding what you want your life to look like in the future. Where do you want to live? What do you want your home to look like? What kind of relationship do you want to have with your children, your spouse, and your neighbors? What kind of shape are you in physically and financially?

Get a journal and write these things down. Get a scrapbook and cut out pictures of all the answers to all these questions. Paste them in the book as if you're in the eighth grade doing a social studies project. Have fun with it. This very act will burn the images into your RAS, and your subconscious mind will start putting the wheels in motion to make these dreams manifest.

When you're writing your goals, make sure that you are very clear and very specific with them. You don't want any of your fearful thoughts to subconsciously draw something to you that you would rather be without. For example, if it is your wish to be married, describe your spouse in detail. Write his or her attributes, passions, goals, and ideals. If you simply jot down, "I want to be married," You might find yourself in a relationship with an abusive spouse or someone that's just not right for you. So be specific.

There was a couple who had been married for thirty years, and on their thirtieth anniversary, a genie appeared to them and told them that he was delighted that they've been together for so long. He went on to state that most marriages never make it past five years, and as a reward for their being together for thirty years, he would grant them one wish each. Whatever they wanted, all they had to do was ask. The wife contemplated her options; she had so many desires. In the thirty years that she'd been married, they'd never been able to afford a vacation. They struggled to finance the children's college education, and their home was dilapidated. She told the genie, "I want to be rich!"

The genie replied, "Listen, you have to be specific! I have been living in a bottle for the past two thousand years. I don't know what rich is, so please be specific."

The wife simplified her instruction, "Please fill the living room with one hundred dollar bills. From the floor to the ceiling, fill it with one hundred dollar notes."

The genie said, "No problem. Your wish is my command."

POOF! When the smoke cleared, there were one hundred dollar notes in the living room from the floor to the ceiling. They were rich.

The genie said to the husband, "Now it's your turn. What do you want?"

The husband looked at the money with excitement in his eyes, and then he looked at his wife. Her hair was dull and grey. He looked at the cash with fascination, and then he looked at his wife. Her face was old and wrinkled. He looked at the money, "I want to be married to someone thirty years younger than I am."

The genie said, "No problem. Your wish is my command." and he made the husband ninety years old. Be specific, or you just might get what you asked for but not what you wanted.

Forest Gump believed that life is like a box of chocolates because you never know what you will get. However, Forest wasn't the brightest bulb on the porch. He was a character of room temperature IQ. If you stood close to him, you could hear the ocean. Life is more like taking a trip on a commercial airline carrier. When you show up at the airport, to get to your destination, you have to check-in. Not only do you have to check-in, but you also have to declare where you are going. If you don't check-in and make that declaration, even though you are at the airport, you don't go anywhere.

Checking in and making your declaration is what you're doing with your journal and scrapbook. Most people spend all their lives at the airport, never checked in, then at sixty-five, they declare, "This is not where I wanted to be."

Checking in is simple, and it's easy. For God's sake, better yet, for your sake, please check-in. Let's use the example that you're in New York, and you've checked in and declared that you're going to LA. Just by making that declaration, you also, by default, declared that you're NOT going to Boston, that you're NOT going to Chicago, and you're NOT going to Miami. You've just decided that even though there may be a million and one other cities to visit, today they are not on your agenda. This is extremely important because people will come along and show you beautiful brochures of the nightlife in Vegas and the beautiful beaches of Miami. They will try to get you to go where they are going. Stay on your agenda! Stay on your flight. You know where you are going. Leave the frivolous tours to those who are on vacation; you're on business.

There are two sides to every coin. On one side, you've decided that you're going to live a purpose-driven life. On the flip side, you've also decided that you are not going to allow friends and family to deter you. This is known in the spiritual world as The Law of Sacrifice. One thing is always going to have to be sacrificed for another. In other words, if you want a happy and faithful marriage, a life of loose living is going to have to be sacrificed for your marriage, or your marriage will be sacrificed for a life of loose living. If greatness is your desire, you're either going to have to sacrifice the undisciplined life for greatness, or you will forfeit your greatness for the undisciplined life. You are not going to spend your weeknights in front of the television. You're not going to spend all your weekends at the club. You are not going to squander your money on meaningless trinkets that society holds sacred, and you're certainly not going to entertain toxic relationships.

While you're checking in, you will be asked, "How many bags are you checking?" Most airlines (before 9/11) allowed you two pieces, anything more than that, and they charged you. The same thing in life; show up like you're Erykah Badu on your way to do a "Bag Lady' video shoot, and you will be severely taxed. In other words, you must leave most of your issues at the door. You must be able to drop the baggage of the past, the baggage of resentment, the baggage of needing to fit in, the baggage of insecurities. Too much baggage causes us to become distracted. Remain distracted long enough, and you're delayed. Remain delayed long enough, and you're denied! You'll be sixty-five in the airport complaining that you weren't breastfed long enough. Release that baggage, and let's go. If you stop labeling everything that happens in your life and learn to view it all as a learning experience, it will become much easier to forgive. Always question life from an empowered point of view, always ask, "What is the lesson that life is trying to teach me here?" With that attitude, you're never a victim, and with that attitude, the tumultuous waters of life now become a joy to navigate.

One interesting fact about the whole baggage situation is that you can show up with only one piece of luggage, and life will still charge you. Do you know why? Because that baggage is overweight. You might show up with only your insecurities, but too much of the same issue and life will tax you. You can't get on the plane with that, so be sure that you are constantly monitoring your thoughts for excess baggage. Also, the more emotional weight that you're carrying, the longer you're going to have to wait for the life of your dreams to unfold.

It is possible that you could have the majority of your house in order and still be denied. Let's assume that you're persistent, you're diligent, you're resilient, but you're traveling with a great deal of self-doubt. That one piece of luggage is enough to get you distracted, delayed, and denied. The more baggage that you show up with, the more it slows you down. The less baggage that you have, the faster you will be able to move, and the quicker you'll accomplish your dreams.

Ridding yourself of your baggage doesn't happen overnight. There's a study that indicates that most Americans spend 30 years of their lives being mad at a family member. It is quite possible to live your entire life and not be aware that you're carrying these burdens with you. We have the uncanny ability to see other people's baggage immediately, but for some reason, the presence of ours seems to escape us. What we can see in someone else within ten minutes of meeting them, we might go a lifetime without seeing in ourselves, because it is challenging to see the picture when you're in the frame.

I hated judgmental people. I detested them like a sickness. It always left me very agitated, hearing someone making assumptions and passing judgment on another individual. I was expressing this to a friend once, and she stopped me mid-sentence and said, 'Kirk, what are you talking about? You are the most judgmental person that I know."

"Huh, what are you kidding me?"

"No, I'm not Kirk, think about it. Who do you know that is more judgmental than you?"

This young lady was a trusted friend with no ulterior motives, and I would rely on her to show me my blind spots. As she revisited example after example, I realize how intolerant I'd been and made a conscious commitment to monitor my thoughts and improve my character. Being able to listen to critical feedback and making the necessary adjustments (while suspending the ego) is one the quickest ways to climb the ladder of self-development.

To rid ourselves of excess baggage is going to take work. It is going to warrant a hard look at the things and emotional triggers that have brought us to our comfort zone. We are going to have to find a way to forgive the people that we've felt caused us pain, and we're going have to forgive ourselves for the pain that we've inflicted. Don't delude yourself into believing that you'll accomplish this in a day. Life is a journey, and it takes constant vigilance and consistent monitoring of our thoughts to arrive at our desired results.

If you want to live, you're going to have to learn how to love, and by God, you're going to have to learn how to forgive. Forgiveness doesn't always come easy. It takes great strength to forgive. The weak can never forgive; forgiveness is an attribute of the strong. The ego loves to hold on to petty slights, and this gives it power. It allows the ego to inflict guilt on the offending party by continually reminding them of what they've done to us. We hold our parents guilty for things that they did over forty years ago. We blame others for our insecurities. Forgiveness allows us to release the other party and take full responsibility for our lives. Your ego will tell you that you have a legitimate claim against the offending party, and the fact is, you might, however, this claim neither serves nor empower you, so release it.

Remember that wherever you are in life right now is the result of your best thinking. Even though you might have made some unreasonable decisions in the past, at the time of making the decision, it was the best decision for that moment. Keep in mind that the people who have caused you pain were using their best thinking as well. Regardless of how much you fume about it, it will not change the past. Irrespective of how much you would like them to acknowledge the insensitivity of their actions, the fact remains that such a thing is out of your control.

Some will, and some won't let it go. We don't get ulcers from what we eat; we get ulcers from what's eating us. Even if you can't get to that place of forgiveness right now, tell yourself that you intend to forgive this person and drop this baggage. Keep reminding yourself of this. Lie to yourself if you must. You've been doing it all your life, by telling yourself that you're not good at this, and you're horrible at that, so why not positively lie to yourself for a change? It works, I guarantee it.

I accidentally stumbled into the power of lying to myself around the age of nineteen. Back then, I suffered from very low self-esteem and self-worth. I didn't believe that I was worthy of being loved, and when I looked into the mirror, I was almost repulsed by the reflection. I was working at a retail electronics chain as a salesman and was instructed to answer the phone by stating the name of the company, the department that the caller had reached, and finally, identify myself to the caller. One day the phone rang, and as a goof, I answered the phone, "Thank you for calling Tops Appliance City, Electronics Department, this is the good looking black man. How may I help you?"

The caller chuckled. She said, "Excuse me, who is this?"

I responded, "Kirk Nugent, the good looking black man."

"Ok, Mr. Good looking black man, do you guys sell portable compact disc players?"

"We certainly do."

"I'll be in later to get one, will you help me when I get there?"

"Of course, just ask for the good looking black man."

She laughed as she hung up. The store manager overheard the conversation as he was walking by and just looked at me and shook his head with a smirk on his face. Two hours later, a young lady entered the store and happened to walk by the manager. He greeted her and asked her if he could be of any assistance. She answered, "I'm here to see the good looking black man."

He smiled, "You must be referring to Kirk Nugent. You'll find him in the Electronics department."

Observing that I was the only black male on the sales floor, she exclaimed, "You must be the good looking black man."

I jokingly replied, "Flesh and blood did not reveal this to you, but my Father which is in heaven did. Indeed I am."

We had so much fun joking about the name that I gave myself that I decided to continue saying it. That scenario continued for the next eighteen months that I worked there. Dozens of times per day I would answer the phone, "Kirk Nugent, good looking black man." and customers would come in asking for the good looking black man.

I unconsciously started updating my suits, placing more starch in my white shirts. I joined a gym and worked out regularly. I carried myself in a manner that was congruent with being "The good looking black man." One day I looked into the mirror, and I was no longer that skinny, scrawny kid that repulsed me. I was a young man that was chiseled, cut like an action figure. I was indeed Kirk Nugent, the good looking black man.

The mere act of me repeating to myself that I am good looking changed the perception that I held of myself. It changed the perception that the world held of me. Remember Muhammad Ali, "I am the greatest"? Today Ali is known as the greatest of all time. A lie repeated enough times will take root into the subconscious, and there, that lie will be transformed into your gospel. Remember, it doesn't have to be true for you to believe it; you only need to believe it for it to become true for you.

In the book of Joel, the Bible instructs, "Let the weak say, I am strong." Unfortunately, we accept the lies that enslave us so easily but struggle to accept the ones that will emancipate us. Bob Marley reminded us to "Emancipate yourself from mental slavery, none but ourselves can free our mind." Lie your way out of this prison called the comfort zone if you must. The goal is freedom by any means necessary. The Bible teaches that there is life and death in the tongue, so start using your tongue to speak the life that you want into existence. "Thou shall declare a thing, and it shall be established unto thee." What have you been establishing with the power of your words?

Begin now by speaking what you want into existence. Your words are that powerful, especially when they're filled with emotions. Start speaking to yourself and tell yourself that you're blessed and highly favored. Tell yourself that things always work out for the best. Never say things such as, "With my luck that will never work."

Change that negative into a positive, tell yourself, "With my luck, it will certainly work out." Whenever something great happens in your life, re-enforce the idea by telling yourself, "Good things always happen to me. That's just how life works for me." Make a habit of speaking blessings into your life. Always use your words to liberate you, never to ensnare, or enslave you. Diligently look for the blessings in your life. Whatever you seek, you will find. The words that you speak will eventually become flesh, and it will dwell among you. Make sure that you're inviting welcomed guests into your home.

Now let's get back to the airport and the business of baggage. Usually, whenever we take a trip, be it business or pleasure, our luggage is actually something that we want to take with us. Be it that favorite business suit, your most comfortable pair of slacks, or your best pair of shoes. For this analogy, let's look at luggage in a more positive light. Let's assume that the luggage that you wanted to take with you are your dreams, your goals, and your ideals. In short, your most intimate desires.

Before September 11, 2001, there were three questions that you had to answer correctly regarding your luggage (dreams) before you would be cleared to head to your destination. If you answered the question incorrectly, you would be delayed and sometimes even denied. Question number one: Did you pack your luggage yourself?

In other words, are these your dreams? The place that you're trying to get to is that your vision or is this what society told you that you ought to be? If you didn't pack your bags yourself, at some point, you'll open them up and find that this is not what you wanted to bring along. These shoes (career, relationship, etc...) don't fit, so now you have to re-pack, and once again, you're delayed and could quite possibly be denied. Are you a relationship and planning to get married because this is what your heart is telling you to do? Or are you trying to fulfill your parent's dreams of having grandchildren before they die?

My dad and all of his brothers are mechanics. When I turned seventeen, he wanted to teach me the trade and was very upset when I told him that I had no interest in learning how to fix cars. He insisted that everyone needed to know how to fix a car and inquired what I would do when my car broke down (as if having a malfunctioning car was inevitable). How would I know if the mechanics were ripping me off? I assured him that my car would never break down. After all, I intended to be wealthy, and all the broken down cars that I ever saw were owned by people dealing with financial challenges. If I had an emergency on the side of the highway, I would simply call AAA to get the car and a limousine service to get me. Besides, I'm a Scorpio; my hands are for caressing and making love, not fondling some greasy engine. God did not call me to repeat someone else's success. He said, "I will do a new thing in you." I don't believe that I was created so that my dad could live vicariously through me. Call me crazy, but I believe that I am here for something other than excelling at mechanical work. I am Kirk Nugent baby, I came here to shine, not to linger in the shadows of some parent's expectations.

Later in life, I found out that my dad wanted to be a musician, but by then, he had a wife and three kids, so he chose to do something more practical. No wonder he was always so irritable and angry. I will do practical things in the grave, but while I'm living, I dare to be an uncommon man. I have found that practicality is the most traveled road to mediocrity.

Even though I was born in Jamaica, where reggae music dominated the airwaves, the words of Frank Sinatra resonated with my soul. In one of his ballads, he was reflecting on his life, and though he made some mistakes along the way, he found comfort in the fact that he did it his way. He was willing to take full responsibility for all that he had encountered and all that he had become. He stood tall and faced it all and did it his way. In my opinion, doing it your way is the only way to do it. Doing it someone else's way is the way of the sheep, and sheep were created for one purpose and one purpose only; that is to be slaughtered. Don't be a sheep, do it your way, without hesitation or reservation, do it boldly, do it beautifully, and do it without apology. Like Ray Charles, you're here to make it do what it do.

Second question: Have your bags been in your possession the entire time? Have you taken your eyes off your dreams? Have you been diligent with your dreams? If you've taken your eyes off your luggage (dreams) and started looking at someone else's, you will be delayed. If you start thinking that I love being a clown, but med school will give me more security, you've just taken your eyes off your luggage. The reason why this question is fundamental is that if you've taken your eyes off your luggage (dreams), you could quite possibly endanger the lives of the pilot and everyone else on the aircraft.

If you've taken your eyes off your dreams, you will be left with a void in your soul. Whatever you use to fill that void, will not bring you any joy, only the dream can fill that void. So now you're a physician with your private practice. However, it's no fun. You're not very attentive to your patients, and you will do just the minimum to get by. You will have no interest in doing further research and staying abreast of the new developments in medicine and treatments. This lack of passion will affect your patients, and it will eventually spill over into your relationships. It will ultimately affect every area of your life and those who are involved with you. Be sure not to lose sight of your luggage.

Third question: Has any unknown person asked you to take anything aboard? The keyword in this question is unknown. What have you picked up subconsciously? Are you receiving messages from the media, friends, and relatives that subconsciously dissuade you from pursuing your career as a clown? How often do you check to make sure that your thoughts and ideas are your own? Do you dislike people of another race or nationality because you were told that this is the patriotic thing to do? Did somehow, along the way, you pick up a program that gave you the impression that being a doctor is more prestigious than being a clown? Do you have an application running, instructing you that it is better to find a spouse in your ethnic group that you have no feelings for than to marry someone outside your race that you're absolutely in love with?

All these issues must be addressed if you desire to navigate your own course. In the scriptures, we are reminded not to be conformed to this world but to be transformed by the renewing of our minds. Don't be so quick to accept the programs that are given to you. If you want the results that everyone is experiencing, then do the things that everyone is doing. Think about the popular and accepted thoughts of the world, and you will certainly end up like every other mediocre person roaming the planet in search of their one lucky break. You can always follow the crowd, but rest assured, you will never be followed by a crowd. The only way to make your mark is to renew your mind with some better information. Renew your mind with truth. All human beings, regardless of race, creed, or culture, are 99.9% similar in genetic structure. Never fall victim to the thinking that tells us that .1% difference far outweighs the 99.9% similarity. Renew your mind, get on board, and let's go. A wonderful life awaits.

Now it's time to board the plane. You're allowed to bring two small carry-ons with you. These are your most personal items that you cannot afford to be without in case the airline misplaces your luggage. You carry on the dreams and ideas that are closest to your heart. You are instructed to place them either in the compartment above your head or under the seat located directly in front of you. Basically, you're being instructed to keep these personal dreams on your mind (above your head) or in your line of vision (in front of you) at all times.

Once you're comfortably seated with your eyes on the prize, you're instructed to fasten your seat belt. Buckle up because this ride could get a little bumpy. We all hope to have a smooth flight, a journey that is free of turbulence and setbacks. We all hope for a flight free of trials and tribulations, tests and testimonies; however, no one can guarantee it. We can't guarantee that there won't be disappointments and heartbreaks. We would love to assure you that there won't be any storms or bumps in the road of life. What we can assure you is that if you keep pressing forward, if you stay the course, if you persist despite the storm, eventually, that plane will land at your destination. It is possible that the flight might be delayed because of bad weather. It is possible that you might be in the vicinity of your goal, but for one reason or another, air traffic control might have you circling in a holding pattern. You could land and get to the gate, but, because of an understaffed ground crew, your luggage might be delayed. There are a million and one variables that could hinder you but, if you stay the course, monitor your thoughts, and act accordingly, I guarantee you that you will not be denied. Life is not about waiting for the storm to pass, but rather learning to dance in the rain.

CHAPTER 4

CHOOSING TO LIVE

"The greatest wealth is health."
Unknown.

A local magazine once interviewed the oldest man in their town on his 105th birthday. They asked him if there were anything in his life that he would've done differently. He thought about it for a minute and then replied, "Had I know I was going to live this long, I would've taken better care of myself."

Most people are so terrified of death that they never give it any conscious thought. They've never decided how long they intend to be here. I know that you're thinking, "No one can predict how long they're going to live." Maybe, but think about this; if you never gave any thought to how long you intend to live then, you'll go through the day by putting anything and everything into your body as long as it gives you immediate comfort and pleasure. However, If you've decided that you intend to be here until the age of one hundred and five, even though there is no guarantee, just by entertaining that thought, you will be more vigilant of what goes into your body and who stays in your life.

You will know that all the sugar that you're consuming will eventually lead to diabetes, and no one with diabetes ever lived to one hundred and five, so you'll make healthier choices. Incidentally, over twenty-one million Americans have diabetes. The Center for Disease Control and Prevention anticipates that one out of every three children born in the United States one will develop diabetes. Diabetes causes heart attacks, stroke, kidney failure, blindness, loss of circulation leading to gangrene, and amputation of feet, legs, and hands. It destroys the nervous system, leaving people in continuous, excruciating pain, and it robs them of the power to fight off infectious disease. Less than twelve percent of people with diabetes inherit the disease. For everybody else who has it, this deadly disease is preventable.

The truth is, there is little or no money to be made from keeping people healthy. There is no money to be made in curing any illness. The money is made by getting children addicted to sugar, sodas, donuts, candy, and all the wrong foods at an early age. This leads them down the path of self-destruction and then thirty or forty years later attaches them to a dialysis machine and financially bleed them until there's nothing left. The money is in the treatment, not the cure, so big corporations have a vested interest in keeping you addicted to an unhealthy lifestyle. Choose to live by keeping as many toxins as possible out of your bodies and out of your life. Investigate the benefits of oil-pulling. It's a simple exercise that will remove tremendous amounts of toxins from your body if practiced on a regular and consistent basis. Join a gym that has either a steam room or a dry sauna (preferably both) and begin removing toxins regularly. Your skin will appear more youthful; your body will be more relaxed, and your immune system will be given a considerable boost.

The number of people getting cancer has increased from 1 in 33 in 1900 to 1 in 2.5 people today. It is estimated that in about 20 years, 1 in 2 people will be diagnosed with cancer, and half of them will die. The most widely used toxin in the world is food. Improper food consumption is the number one cause of illness in the world and accounts for more deaths than World War I and II combined. There has been much research and conclusive evidence on how sugar systematically destroys and breaks down the organs of the body. Yet, Americans consume fifteen billion gallons of soda per year. That's five hundred and sixty cans per person per year.

My purpose for writing this book is not to give you a long drawn out lecture on diet, but rather to help you realize that if you desire to be here for a while, then you might as well start acting like it. It doesn't make sense to want a long healthy life while you go about your day systematically sabotaging your body and your mind. We're living in the information age, so take the time to find out what the body needs to support your goals and feed it foods that are compatible with your desires. Go to www.youtube.com/kirknugent and watch my video series on, Health Care and also on, The Magic of Believing. There you will find instructions on how to take simple steps to drastically improve your life.

As a child growing up in Jamaica, afflicted with Sickle Cell Anemia, the doctors predicted that I would be dead by age thirteen. Upon my arrival in America, my doctors wanted to place me on permanent disability and have the state take care of me. My doctors' vision of my future was not in alignment with the greatness that I desired. I refused the government's handout and went off in search of my passion. I didn't do any of the teenage stuff to jeopardize my life. I didn't drink; I didn't smoke, and I didn't do drugs, be it prescription or over the counter. I must admit that I had a severe sugar addiction, and to this day, I have to be vigilant of my sugar intake. I must continuously remind myself, "Kirk, nothing tastes as great as good health feels." If you want to live longer than the average person, then you must do things that the average person will not do.

Ask yourself, are you committed to being here? Bear in mind that our level of commitment will always show up in our actions. Just about everyone reading this book has heard the general instructions for longevity. Eat plenty of fruits and vegetables, exercise, and keep your body properly hydrated. Simple directions, yet when it comes to adhering to them, most people are seriously not serious. By asking yourself, how long do I intend to be here, you shift your focus into being more proactive with your health. You will become more responsible for your health because your expectations will have changed. So instead of running around subconsciously poisoning your body, looking for ingenious ways to derail your life, you'll start to look consciously for ways to stay alive. You will begin to develop the habit patterns that are conducive to the thought of being here for a very long time.

I don't like the taste of vegetables. For some reason, they don't resonate with my taste buds. I do understand how vital they are to my longevity, so I bought a juicer, and every morning I have a big veggie cocktail. They don't taste any better juiced, but at least I can get it down in several gulps and be on my way. Ice cream, on the other hand, I thoroughly enjoy, but I am also aware of the dangers of dairy, so ice cream has been scaled back to infrequent occasions. It's a system of balance that I can live with (pun intended).

The majority of the foods that are a part of the American diet are highly toxic and acidic. These toxins serve only to destroy our organs and arrest our immune system. They are biological time bombs waiting to explode inside of us. Waiting to detonate and discharge shrapnel of cancer all through our temple. Just as toxic foods are destructive and disastrous to our bodies, toxic people are disruptive and devastating to our spirit.

My mentor Les Brown refers to toxic people as energy drainers, and that is true. Your body will go weak in their presence. He told me that some people are so negative that if you placed them in a dark room, they would start to develop. These are the people in your life that seem to be blessed with the clairvoyant ability to know what you can or cannot accomplish. Fortunately for us, toxic people are too small to be mediums. They're always reminding you of your past failures and previous defeats. They strive to keep you in your comfort zone. They never encourage you to stretch; instead, they always see the risk involved in any venture.

Some people are like a shadow, they're only with you when the sun is shining, and they can never see your greatness until others in the world have affirmed it. These are the people that tiptoe through life, hoping to arrive safely at death. They will poison, pollute, and pervert your passion with their pessimistic plague and pestilence. Toxic people are a crusher of confidence, a cancer to the consciousness, and they are as contagious as the common cold. They're usually generous with their slander and liberal with their insults. Until your spiritual immune system is strong enough not to be infected by them, toxic people should be avoided at all costs.

If the relationship is not serving you, end it and open yourself up to more desirable ones. It is better to be by yourself than to wish that you were. Your friends will either stretch your vision or choke your dreams. It is always better to run with an army of allies than a cavalry of critics. There is a proverb that is popular in Jamaica; it says: Show me your company, and I'll tell you who you are. I have also heard it expressed, show me your five closest associates, and I'll show you your future. So the lesson is that we should always be mindful of our relationships, the people who we allow access to our lives and minds. Always be conscious of the energy and vibration of the people that you're around. Be aware of your energy and vibration as well because energies are always entangling and affecting the moods and frequencies of those in proximity to them.

Sidney Poitier, in his book The Measure of a Man, says that a funny thing happens when two people walk down a street together, one adjusts to the pace of another, nothing that we do consciously, but something that we all do. Whenever you're on a higher level of consciousness, it is almost impossible for someone on a lower level of consciousness to rise to your level, but it is not so farfetched for you to gradually sink to theirs.

I can recall being in a relationship where our consciousness wasn't compatible. I was an avid reader. I loved personal development books. I would leave work, get home, and open a book. I read, Think and Grow Rich by Napoleon Hill, How to Win Friends and Influence People by Dale Carnegie, The University of Success by Og Mandino, The Magic of Believing by Claude Bristol and Live your Dreams by Les Brown. You name it, I read it! I never smoked, I never did drugs or alcohol, but I was addicted to Barnes and Noble. I would walk into a bookstore giving myself a pep talk, "Kirk, we're only going to spend twenty dollars, no more Kirk, only twenty dollars." Then I would walk out after investing over two hundred dollars. As soon as I got home, I would meticulously sign each book: Kirk Nugent, born to win, destined to be great."

Somehow I instinctively knew that I was here for something greater than my current circumstances. I knew that somehow, I was here to make a difference. I knew that my life had more meaning than selling electronics for a retail chain. I knew that even in the midst of lack, one day, I would be able to breathe life into the lifeless. I am here to resurrect the spiritually dead, and by God, that's what I'm going to do. I remember being depressed and suicidal, lying on my bed, channel surfing. I stumbled onto a PBS special, and a speaker by the name of Les Brown spoke life back into my soul. He told me that there was greatness inside of me, and I could change my life just by changing my thoughts. I bought wholeheartedly into his philosophy. I took my personal development training seriously because I hoped that one day my words would do the same for someone living in a state of hopelessness. I made the intention that I would be a force for good upon this Earth, and my life would serve to enlighten others. I wanted to be a source of joy and inspiration, moving people from the mundane to the miraculous.

I even confessed my dreams to one of my 'friends' and immediately he shot it down, "Man, you can't be an inspirational speaker, your Jamaican accent would confuse everybody." Fortunately, I didn't allow his opinion of me to become an indictment of me. However, I never spoke to him again regarding any of my dreams. I quietly kept my training regimen going. I started studying other speakers. I bought a notebook and started listing all the interesting facts and statistics that I thought I would one day need for my speeches.

I would go into the bedroom, close the door behind me and begin reading a book. That was my training; the books were boot camp. You can't lead where you don't go, and you can't teach what you don't know. I intimately understood this concept. I figured that if for $19.95 I could get inside the heads of Dale Carnegie, Mark Victor Hansen, Anthony Robbins, Wayne Dyer, Bruce Lipton and, Les Brown, then sooner or later, I would be able to emulate their success.

My partner was not into books. She enjoyed the television, which was her escape. However, she respected my passion for books and never interrupted me while I was reading. She never asked me to join her in the living room. She steadily pursued her passion, and I did the same for mine. Whenever I was reading, I would hear her in the living room, laughing hysterically, having the time of her life. It wasn't long before I started leaving the bedroom door open so that I could keep both eyes on the book and one ear cocked towards the television. Even though I knew that you do not become a millionaire by watching 'Who wants to become a millionaire?' I found myself lending a listening ear to what was going on in the living room rather than giving my undivided attention to my studies.

A few months went by, and now I was reading in the kitchen as opposed to the bedroom. Subconsciously I was drawing closer to the TV. Even though I knew my purpose, even though I was focused on my vision, the environment that I was living in was beginning to mold me. After a while, I would sit at the kitchen table with the book open, but I would be watching the television in the living room and only reading during the commercial breaks.

What is interesting about this story is that at no point did she stop watching television and begin reading. She stayed on her agenda. I, on the other hand, got on hers. In the words of Sidney Poitier, I adjusted to her pace. If you walk with the lame, eventually, you will develop a limp, so whose pace have you been adjusting to? What have you picked up subconsciously that is keeping you away from your greatness? It was much easier for me to slide down to her level than for her to climb to mine. I'm not here to make judgment calls by saying reading a book is more important than watching television. That's not what the illustration is about. The point is, whatever your goals are, be mindful of your environment and your relationships. Make sure that they are conducive to your goals.

Sometimes you will find yourself in situations where you won't be able to immediately change your environment; these are the times when you need to be most vigilant of your habits. Make sure that your habits and your goals are in perfect alignment. Think of everything and everyone in your life as a teacher. If you're constantly looking for the lesson, you'll never blame the teacher; you'll be grateful for the lesson. I had a few relationships that didn't work, but instead of finding fault and becoming judgmental, I asked, "What's the lesson here? What is life trying to teach me?" I understand that the faster I learn and apply the lesson, the sooner I graduate to the next level.

Continually evaluate your actions to make sure that you haven't started adjusting to someone's pace that is not walking in the direction that you want to go. There was a study conducted which concluded that the average American socially interacts with people who earn within ten thousand dollars plus or minus of their income. These are people who cannot challenge you because they're seeing the same view that you're observing.

One of the reasons why Americans watch over twenty-nine hours of television per week is because most Americans have no goals. People without goals need to be constantly entertained. You can tell them by their motto, "I am bored." They need constant stimulus to distract them from the fruitless life that they're producing, so they get lost in voting for the next American Idol, and they need to be kept abreast of what is going on in the tribunals of Survivor. Successful people plan for generations; unsuccessful people plan for Saturday night.

It is impossible for people who are striving for something more significant to be bored. They're busy trying to figure out how to get to that next level, how to overcome a present challenge, how to grow, and get the best out of their current situation. People who are destined for greatness are seldom bored. They understand that boredom is a sign from life, signaling them that they're off course. Bored people are always in search of the next distraction. They tend to be very uncomfortable with the idea of merely spending time with themselves and just being. These are the sleeping souls that attempt to interrupt your life with trivial phone calls beginning with, "Oh, I'm just calling to see what you're doing, I didn't want anything. I was just bored, so I decided to give you a call."

Whenever I told my friends and relatives of my glorious dreams, they would laugh. My eldest sister even told me, "Kirk, you're always dreaming, telling me about what you're going to do. Talk to me when you've done it." They could not see me accomplishing the ideals that I'd set for myself from where they're standing. From their vantage point, those were impossible ideals; however, upon meeting Les Brown and sharing my dreams, he laughed as well, except he was coming from a different perspective.

He said, "Kirk, you have to set bigger goals than those. You will accomplish those goals in a few years, set some goals that will make you stretch; there is greatness within you."

Get out and network. Meet and greet people who will help you grow, and you can help them grow. Avoid the unhappy and the unlucky, for their disease is contagious, infectious, and insidious. Always look for serendipitous situations, let the dead bury the dead, leave them with the dread, the uncertainty, and the distrust because a life of mediocrity is not your destiny. Don't allow someone's toxic thoughts to seep under your skin, get into your veins, and pollute your bloodstream. They will have your heart pumping fear, doubt, and insecurities instead of faith, hope, and confidence. Your mind will start manufacturing recipes for failure, prescriptions for procrastination. You'll lose that glimmer in your eye, and when we meet on the road of life, I'll recognize you as just another dead person walking.

Toxic people serve to develop a divide and disconnect between you and the God within you. Entertain them long enough, and through the process of osmosis, you'll soon start to become cynical and critical. You'll begin to self-medicate with prescription drugs and alcohol, using cocaine to numb the pain while Marlboro helps you make it to tomorrow. Television becomes another source of escape, so now you live vicariously through the characters. Whenever your favorite sports team wins a game, you declare, "We won!" However, they're living their dreams, and you're not. They're getting paid to play, and you're not. We didn't win, they did, and at the end of the month, they don't have to come up with the mortgage, you do.

One of the reasons why it is so critical to avoid the company of toxic people (let the dead bury the dead), is because they're usually thin-skinned and easily offended. Their egos are as fragile as eggshells, and you never know what will offend them. It's an emotional chore trying to keep them happy as you begin to second guess your every action and word.

Years ago, one of my co-workers told me that he had a million-dollar idea. I immediately replied, "Act on it," however, he became upset and was convinced that I did not believe in his idea because I was not curious about the details of the concept. I asked him, "Is it possible that you're the one who doesn't believe in your idea, and you feel an overwhelming need to sell me on the idea so that in the process, you can sell yourself?"

Here is what I know. I know that men have made millions of dollars marketing anything from Pet Rocks to Cabbage Patch Dolls. I know empires that have been built upon ideas that were as ridiculous as the Chia Pet, and I've known men that were so talented that the Jackson Five would drown in their gene pool, yet they were starving to death. The point is, the idea is irrelevant, but the ability to act on that idea with conviction will make all the difference in the world. If my reluctance to ask him to elaborate on his idea is enough to deter him, then his idea was doomed before he presented it to me.

Someone walking around nursing old wounds and deep-seated insecurities will always come across as unbalanced. They're in victim consciousness and are looking to attack the world before they're attacked. Their egos are easily bruised, and it is best to let them be. People with unresolved issues are usually walking around wounded, and they attack if you come within a predetermined proximity of that wound. The only problem is that until you get to know them, you can never be sure where their emotional land mines are buried. The landscape of their mind is one colossal battlefield wired with booby traps, barbed wire, claymore mines, and C4 explosive charges. My advice would be to stay clear.

There was a woman that I thoroughly loved. No one could've convinced me that I was not going to marry this woman. When I gazed upon her, she would always inquire, "What are you staring at?" When God created her, he was having the time of His life. She was His meticulous commitment to craftsmanship. She was beautifully rendered and flawlessly finished; she was visually arresting. Not to stare would be an insult. She was an offer worth investigating, and I was drawn to her frame like fire to a flame. Her sweetness was indeed my weakness.

Our conversations were more like a spiritual dance. We discussed the magnificent and the mundane as we engaged in intellectual foreplay. I told all my friends of my intentions to marry her, and I moved from New Jersey to Florida to be closer to her. Our relationship was beautiful. We spent blissful hours on the beach enjoying the beautiful Floridian sunsets. She was working full time and going back to University at night to earn her degree. I admired her ambition.

We would go to see Anita Baker and Beres Hammond in concert. We both loved to laugh, so we would go to The Improv and have the time of our lives. We both shared a Caribbean heritage, so we enjoyed the same music and the same foods. On Friday nights, we would go to the Jamaican restaurant and stuff ourselves with steamed snapper, jerk chicken, and roast breadfruit, while listening to Bob Marley and Buju Banton drop some serious reggae. She was, without a doubt, the missing variable in my perfect equation.

There was only one source of tension. Whenever we disagreed, she became belligerent. She would yell and curse; her entire physiology would become tensed as she prepared for an all-out war. She became very disrespectful and said things that she would later claim to regret. She argued with unusual tenacity. Her verbiage was vulgar, her vernacular, vile and vicious. Her dialogue was demeaning, debasing, and degrading. She held onto the emotional residue of what I considered to be a petty misunderstanding for days, sometimes weeks. I knew that she was not lashing out at me, but instead, she was still hanging on to the pain of past hurt, so she painted with a broad brush and took no prisoners. Her issues were seldom with me, but they were always with Black men, and though I'm trying to be more Christ-like, I felt no need to be crucified for the perceived sins of a race of men.

I grew up in a household where my dad would come home and go into one of his tirades. He would become extremely combative as he yelled at us for what seemed like hours at a time. His words would lacerate our pride, and my mom, broken from the stress, would in turn, emotionally berate us. The environment was so deeply depressing and toxic that I made a conscious decision that such a lifestyle would not work for me. I would not argue; it brought me no joy. Arguments sap the very energy of my soul, and even though I am by no means a pacifist, my first instinct is always to walk away. If we can't calmly talk our way through our differences at this moment, then let's just be silent for a while and discuss it later. She interpreted my silence to be indifference, which only served to ignite her anger and fuel her fire. I was aware that the person who does not understand your silence very seldom understood your words. So I was very adamant in my decision not to be disrespectful; however, I was equally steadfast in my decision not to be disrespected.

I explained to 'Baby' in no uncertain terms; I said, "Baby, I am not going to tolerate your incivility. Either you choose to gain control over your tongue, or I will choose to be someplace where I won't have to hear your tongue."

She replied, "I can't help it, I get agitated, and then stuff just comes out." Her explanation was not only inadequate; it was unacceptable.

I calmly responded, "Baby, to say that you can't help yourself is not a truthful statement. You're upset at your boss a lot, yet you've never cursed or screamed at him. You've never spoken to him with contempt or disdain. You choose to control your tongue because you need that paycheck. If you can learn to control your tongue for a paycheck that has no feeling, is it possible that you could exercise the same level of control over it for a feeling, caring human being?"

I understand that a relationship is all about compromise, but me being treated with a certain level of dignity was non-negotiable. I believe in going where I am celebrated, not where I am tolerated. In the end, she chose not to mince her words; I chose not to be minced by her words.

It's been years since I've been keeping that commitment. I will not allow myself to be dragged into an argument. Life is too short and unpredictable for me to make myself available for hellish experiences. If someone wants to argue, that's fine, but they need to find another playmate to attend that argument. I understand that I don't have to attend every party that I'm invited to, and I certainly don't have to attend every argument that beckons.

Start isolating and insulating yourself from these toxic energies and life will begin to take on a whole new luster. You will start to see the possibilities that you've never seen before. At the same time, be sure that you're not a toxic force in someone else's life. Always be an encourager, find ways to lift the people who you've decided to be in your life. Allow others to make their mistakes and grow at their rate. Too often, we tear people down in the process of trying to build them up.

Choose to see the greatness in yourself and others. Even if they're not on your level, realize that this is where they choose to be, and when they're ready, they will choose something different. Unfortunately, we want people to choose something different when it's convenient for us. We are all growing, so don't set out trying to change others who are perfectly comfortable in their ways, just be the change that you wish to see in the world.

DESTINY

I'm the One, born under the sign of Scorpio,
I wrote this poem so you would know
That your fears be phony like Ms. Cleo.
"Call me now!" and I won't ask you,
"Who is that man in your house?"
I'll show you who is that God in your heart,
I'll show you who is that giant within,
I'll show you that you were born to win
And it is your fears that make you a victim.

You don't even have to be, "Bout it, 'bout it."
I am here to show you that you're a No Limit Soldier.
I am here to show you that life is a mirror,
It can only reflect you.
So, in short, I will show you that life is perfect truth!

Today I set before you a blessing and a curse,
Today I give you the powers to govern your own universe.
Because by our words, we're justified, by our words, we're condemned.
Behold the knowledge that I send and be careful what you speak,
The vibrations of your thoughts will elevate you above the highest peak
Or it will bring you to come crashing to your knees.
Ever notice that women who complain that,
"All men are dogs." Always seem to wake up with fleas?

It is that simple:
My thoughts control my destiny.
So tell my enemies
They can no longer get the best of me
For today I'm here to claim my destiny.

I've come to claim my birthright,
What is rightfully mine,
What was given to me from the Divine.
Today I'm here to let my light shine.
So I'm rolling up my sleeves
And I'm gritting my teeth
And I dare Life to try and derail my dreams.

For I've been these trenches for centuries,
Paid my dues, never made a fuss.
I've labored long, and I've suffered much,
But today I'm lacing up my boots,
I've got my mouthpiece in.
Somebody put my music on I'm
making my way to the ring.
Go tell that dirty Devil that Kirk Nugent said,
"Not today baby, not today!"
You just ain't breaking me today!
I don't care if you hit me with heartaches,
Headaches and bills that are unpaid!
You're just not defeating me today.

Today I refuse to be broken,
I will not be denied!
Ain't nobody turning me around
And the same ain't bringing me down.
So you can step aside with you snide remarks and your belittling words
Your lying lips no longer hurt.
I will no longer deny who I am, just to be accepted by you.
No more will I tolerate you in my space
With that constant frown
Bringing my spirits down.
When you approach me,
Take off thy shoes for you're standing on holy ground.

For today I'm shedding my limitations,
Erasing my boundaries,

Removing borders and expanding frontiers.
Fear and failure can no longer flourish here.
I am here to pay the price and walk away with my Destiny
And from this stage, I will boldly state it,
I will not bow,
I will not buckle
And I will not be intimidated!

Today I am swimming out to meet my ship before it docks,
Today I am walking away from the flock,
No more tears to weep, no more poor little me
I am walking away from the sheep.
For I am a lion!
And I refuse to eat, to sleep, to sit with the sheep.
I am defiant.
Five-foot ten, a hundred and fifty five-pound giant.
And I do not fit among little people
With their little people's problems, and their little people's fear.
Tell me nothing of my limitations, all I see are possibilities
For I am connected to Source, and Life simply cannot break me.

Today I will run and not be weary,
Walk and not faint,
Persistence and tenacity ain't got nothing on me
As a matter of fact, I'm telling 2003 to 2093
Exactly what they're gonna do for me!
For I will not be moved,
Like DNA I am living proof
That Life cannot battle against the sword of my spirit,
Not when everything in my life is relative
Even my blood type is B positive.

Self-pity has long lost her allure,
I told you, I Don't Write About Depression No More

I am far from fragile, did not get out of bed this morning to fail,
I'm the best pound for pound
And certainly did not get dressed just to be turned around.
The turbulence doesn't terrify me
Tell the thunder, be gone.
I might be at the end of my rope, but I'm tying a knot
And By God, I'm holding on!
I'm in the eye of the storm with no life vest; shipwrecked.
But today I'm treading water; I'm kicking in doors
I'm just not swallowing this saltwater no more.
If Life thinks that spiritually it can break me
Then somebody done lied
Because today I will not be swept away with the tide.
Today I will swim with the sharks and not be eaten
Did not spend nine months in the womb,
Just to come out to be beaten.
Ain't nobody turning me around.

I'm not listening to you,
Telling me that I'm ugly,
My skin is dirty, and my cause is unworthy.
Not today baby, not today!
For today I'm here to cast all complaints aside,
Today I am clinging to Life.
I am more than able, beyond capable
I taught Bruce Willis what it meant to be unbreakable
Wherever I sit is the head of the table.

I refuse to collapse in the face of calamity
Bring me your so-called adversity,
And I'll beat that illusion into opportunity.
I am here to claim my destiny.

*Excerpt of the poem 'Destiny" was taken from my previous book, 'Answer The Call.'

CHAPTER 5

PURSUE YOUR PASSION

> "If I could've convinced more slaves
> that they were slaves,
> I would've freed thousands more."
> *Harriet Tubman*

I was twenty-five years young and living the 'American Dream,' which quickly turned into a nightmare. I was working as a salesman for a furniture retail giant in New Jersey, earning around fifty-five thousand per year. The seasoned salespeople in the company were earning somewhere around ninety to one hundred thousand dollars per year. So it was apparent that it would be only a matter of time before I would increase my clientele, forge more significant relationships with my customers, get more referrals, and repeat business. Before the age of thirty, I would be earning one hundred thousand dollars per year. Whoopee! Not only did the job carry great benefits, but the Teamsters Union backed my position, so my job was pretty much secured.

There were only a few drawbacks to the job, none that irritated me. The hours were relatively short for retail sales. We worked no more than forty-eight hours per week. Working holidays was optional, but if you wanted to stay in good graces with the managers, it would be best to consider them mandatory. Besides, holidays were great sales days, so working on those days was never a source of tension. The only painful part of the job was walking the sales floor. I bought a pedometer once and wore it all day. I discovered that I walked over twenty miles, which shocked me because that particular day was considered to be a relatively slow day. The sales floor was not carpeted; it was concrete, so it took an exceptional toll on my flat feet.

I soon developed a heel spur. Before this, I had no idea what a heel spur was. I was in agonizing pain, limping around the sales floor. I told my manager about the pain, and he said that it was probably a heel spur. I left work and went to see a podiatrist. He informed me that indeed I had a heel spur; however, the insurance that my job provided only covered me from the ankle up. I asked, "What does that mean, from the ankle up?" He told me that my insurance didn't cover any ailment that I suffered below my ankle. "Hold on a sec, let me process this. My job is to walk the sales floor, an average of twenty miles per day, and my insurance doesn't cover any injuries to my feet. Is that what you're telling me?"

"That is exactly what I'm telling you. Being that this is your first time here, the cost of your visit is seventy-five dollars; if you would like an injection of cortisone to ease the pain temporarily, that will be an additional one hundred and fifty dollars. Will that be cash or charge?"

I was livid! Twice per week, I had to return to the podiatrist for a sixty dollar visit and a one hundred and fifty dollar injection. Four hundred and twenty dollars deducted from my check, which was barely six hundred dollars after taxes, so now I'm down to less than two hundred dollars per week. To make matters worse, I was still in pain, wasn't able to hustle around the sales floor as effectively as the other salespeople who were running circles around me. My commissions suffered. Within a few weeks, I was earning less than three hundred dollars per week. To add insult to injury, my manager started reprimanding me for not selling as much furniture as the other salespeople. I was carrying the store numbers down. He wrote me up twice; one more and I would be fired. Oh, I was livid! They're laying the foundation to fire me, and there was nothing I could do about it. Who the hell is going to hire me if I can't walk?

Fortunately, it wasn't long before I was fully recovered and entirely bitter. How dare they try to fire me for something beyond my control, for something they probably caused? The job became the bane of my existence. A place that once furnished my joy now seemed to be infested with imbeciles. I felt as though I was being managed by a moron, and the regional office was saturated with simpletons. Did I mention that I was bitter?

I started contemplating what I wanted out of life. I knew that there was nothing unique about my situation. People are losing their pension as I type these words. GM recently downsized its personnel by 30,000 people, and they are planning more cutbacks. By the time you're reading this book, GM could very well be obsolete. However, I was never concerned with job security; I was more concerned with being happy. All the books that I'd read told me that the secret to creating wealth was to find something that I loved and find someone to pay me to do it. I knew that the key was to be committed; after all, one can never steal second base with one foot still on first.

I've always had the feeling that my life was meant to be more than average. I didn't want to die an unlived life, yet being in the place where I spent the majority of my time felt like I was committing spiritual suicide. I lost interest in the job. Instead of waiting on my customers, I instructed them to look around while I sat at my desk and wrote poetry. Pouring my pain from the pen to the paper was therapeutic; the words on the page became a healing balm as I learned how to channel my anger constructively. I knew that I was here for something great, what that something was I didn't know. I also knew that I wanted to help people. I wanted to be an inspirational speaker like Les Brown. His story appealed to me, especially because he wasn't college-trained, and neither was I. He made me see possibilities where I usually saw only obstacles.

As I started sharing my poetry with a few close friends, they all expressed their excitement for my writings and encouraged me to pursue my God-given talent. I came home from work one Saturday night and turned on the television, which was quite unusual. Rarely did I watch tv. Showtime at the Apollo was on, and a poet by the name of Jessica Caremoore was performing her poetry with such intensity and passion that she won five weeks in a row. I thought, "WOW! I can do that! That's what I want to do. That's what I'm going to do. But how do I make the transition from employee to artist without starving to death?"

The idea of being a starving artist did not appeal to me. However, the idea of being a poet and touring the world consumed my thoughts. I started leaving work early on Friday nights and made my way to an open mic in Brooklyn, where I was given three minutes on the microphone. Those were the most blissful three minutes one could ever hope to experience. The more I read my poetry, the more I knew that this is what I came here to do. The more I read my poems, the more difficult it became to return to work on Saturday morning. Whenever I greeted a customer, my demeanor was punctuated by a total lack of interest. The conversation that played in my head while dealing with a customer was, "Look! It's a damn couch, not brain surgery, pick one and let's go." I had a permanent frown chiseled into my personality, a chip on my shoulder, and resentment for my job; however, there was nothing unique about me. This is who we become when we're not living our dreams. We slowly begin to die on the inside, and the lifeless zombie is who we send into the world to interact with all whom we come in contact.

I'm sure that you've met dozens of people like I used to be, I see them all the time at the local DMV. I frolicked in my foolishness while simultaneously cosigning my spiritual demise. By the end of the week, when I received my compensation, emotionally, I was as stable as a trailer park in a tornado. The environment had become sandpaper against my soul. I needed out but did not know how I would survive as an artist.

Divine discontent kept me searching for a way out, and I grew more frustrated with my employment as the days wasted away. I recall a passage that I read in the Bible, which stated, "Ask, and ye shall receive, seek and ye shall find." I kept asking, and I kept on seeking. It's incredible how many ways God finds to speak to us when we're receptive. Unfortunately, we're so wrapped up in the illusion of our problems that we sometimes miss them all. Today was not going to be such a day. I left work and went to a Jamaican restaurant and ordered my usual jerk chicken with rice and peas and two bottles of Ting. As I sipped my refreshing Ting, waiting for my food to be served, a brother from the Nation of Islam approached me. He had a table outside of the restaurant where he sold, "The Final Call," incense, Black literature, and recorded speeches of The Honorable, Minister Louis Farrakhan.

He said, "Young brother, why don't you help me sell some newspapers and start your own business?"

I thought to myself, "Sell some papers?" What is this guy...nuts? I have a good job, making good money, do I look like I need to sell some damn paper? "Naw bro I'm good, appreciate the offer though."

"What do you mean, you're good?"

"I've got a good job!"

"What about after work?"

Damn, this dude is persistent! "Naw son, I don't have time after work. I work retail sales, from ten in the morning to ten at night," exaggerating my schedule; I hoped to end the conversation.

"What about on your day off?"

"Dude, I work six days per week. The day that I'm off is the day that I do my laundry and prepare to get back to work."

"You just do this on your own; no one forces you to do this?"

"Yea?"

"That's a shame!"

"What's a shame?"

"You were born at the wrong time."

Ok, what kind of fortune teller garbage is this cat throwing at me? "What do you mean I was born at the wrong time?"

He looked me square in the eyes and uttered the words that changed the course of my life forever.

"You would've made a good slave!"

"YOU WOULD'VE MADE A GOOD SLAVE!"

The truth of that statement hit like a tidal wave. He was correct. Here I am, a grown man in a free world, yet I allowed myself to be chained to a paycheck, detained by a desk, and held hostage by an HMO. My job was killing my spirit, yet I decided to stay because it was better than the unknown. Harriet Tubman's words echoed in my head like cannons exploding in my soul. "If I could've convinced more slaves that they were slaves, I would've freed thousands more." Until the brother enlightened me, I never realized that I was enslaved, but now that I was aware of it, it was time to escape that plantation.

I paid for my dinner, but by the time I left the restaurant, I had completely lost my appetite. I did not sleep well that night. I was tormented by the truth that I was ashamed to admit. "You would've made a good slave." A good slave! It's one thing being enslaved and mistreated; sometimes, we don't have a choice in such matters. But it's a horse of a different color to cooperate with the treatment. I was assisting in my downfall, and such behavior was unacceptable for this good looking black man. If I had to be a slave, I wanted to be a bad slave. One that would rebel and burn the plantation to the ground, one that would escape or make attempts to escape, incite riots and inflict all manner of pain upon my oppressors. I wanted to be the type of slave that swore his allegiance to freedom and sought her face as passionately as the system fought to keep him in servitude. Instead, here I am, a house negro, steppin' and fetchin' to the beat of a drummer whose music did not resonate with my heart.

I returned to work the next day and saw the plantation with new eyes. I observed everyone, from maid to manager, black and white, young and old, walking around, void of passion, consumed by their circumstances, performing a job that they obviously disdained and despised. They've grown comfortable in their contempt...all good slaves. Uncertain of my next move, I found courage in my culture. Reassured by the words of Bob Marley, "Emancipate yourself from mental slavery, none but ourselves can free our mind."

Jimmy Cliff reminded me, "You can get it if you really want it." He was indifferent to the obstacles that might be on the path to my passion. "The harder they come, the harder they fall one and all." I made a commitment to myself that tonight when I punched this time clock to leave, I would never return. Nor would I trade one plantation for another, one master for another. From this day forward, I will be captain of my soul, master of my fate. Kirk Nugent: Born to win, destined to be great. I concluded that while others have egos to build and inferiority complexities to fight, until the day I die, I've got poems to write. No longer would I be chained to a pension plan. No longer would I be in servitude to a dental package or be bounded by my bills. Let the chips fall where they may, but I am choosing to live.

How many times have we chosen to be enslaved by our fears? How many of us are imprisoned by the opinions of others? What will the neighbors think? Who cares? Someone else's opinion of you is none of your business unless of course, you're running for office. It is not your soul's purpose to live as a slave. You need not wait for a proclamation from Lincoln to declare your emancipation; all you need is the courage to say, "Enough!" Within you lies that power, waiting to be unleashed. Within you lies greatness that sometimes cannot be realized within the confines of a nine to five.

I encourage you to trust the voice inside your heart; it has more wisdom than the voice inside your head. The voice in your head is from all the programming that you've taken on. The limiting thinking, the lack of possibilities, and all the fears of what might go wrong are in your head. Your heart is the source of your intuition; it is the seat of your power...commune with it. Prayer is you, calling God; intuition is God calling back. Your heart will lead you to your passion and your purpose, but very rare is your heart logical, and that's what frightens us. Your heart is an instrument of faith, and faith my friend, is never logical. That's why it is not something to be explained but instead expressed. Being that faith is so illogical, to the untrained eye, a person walking by faith is usually viewed as crazy. So remember, the dream was not given to you so that you could explain it, it was given to you so that you could experience it.

An EMT once told me that most people who die in car accidents are usually found sitting on their seat belts. I thought that was an excellent metaphor for life because too often, we go to our graves with a broken spirit when the one thing (our passion) that could've given us more life (both literally and figuratively) we sat on.

Even relatives started assuming that I was on drugs when I quit my so-called 'good' job. To make matters worse, I never explained myself or my intentions to them. My vision was placed in my heart, not theirs. They were not following their hearts, which meant that they could not see their dreams. Logic dictates that if they can't see their very own dreams, then they damn sure will not be able to see mine, so why bother trying to explain something that they will never see? I encourage you to do the same; keep your dreams and ideas close to your heart. The last thing that you need is for some logical thinker to start casting doubts on your illogical, faith-based, dreams. You did not come here to walk your parent's path; you came to chisel your name on infinity's wall. You were not created to fit in, but rather to stand out, so never allow someone who is not living their dreams to talk you out of yours.

History is comprised of great men and women who stepped out on faith towards their ideals. They weren't concerned with the odds. They weren't perplexed by probabilities or hindered by handicap. Obstacles served to inspire them; mountains motivated them to move forward. They kept looking for new and unique ways to win. They sought out mentors and applied their newfound knowledge with great diligence. The great men and women were fluid and adaptable; they sought opportunities rather than security.

In 1776 Thomas Paine wrote,

"I do not choose to be a common man. It is my right to be uncommon if I can. I seek opportunity, not security. I do not wish to be a kept citizen. Humbled and dulled by having the State look after me. I want to take the calculated risk, to dream and to build, to fail, and to succeed. I refuse to barter incentive for a dole; I prefer the challenges of life to the guaranteed existence; the thrill of fulfillment to the stale calm of Utopia. I will not trade freedom for beneficence nor my dignity for a handout. I will never cower before any master nor bend to any threat. It is my heritage to stand erect, proud and unafraid; to think and act for myself, to enjoy the benefit of my creations and to face the world boldly and say: This, with God's help, I have done."

Those words became my affirmation and my driving force. I would look in the mirror and boldly tell myself, "Kirk Nugent, you did not come here to be a common man; therefore, your path will be uncommon, and your road will be less traveled. Be OK with that." I fed my mind the information that would give me the courage to press on.

Michael Jordan's math teacher told him that he should become a math teacher, because in her words, "That's where the money is." Fortunately, for Mr. Jordan and all his fans, he chose to pursue his passion. What if Dr. Martin Luther King Jr. had played it safe? What if he was concerned for his life? Where would America be today? Could she go abroad and demand democracy when apartheid was erecting tents on her front lawn? Pursue your passion; you cannot begin to contemplate how many lives are directly and indirectly tied to you being fruitful with your vision.

According to People magazine, Oprah had a 1-in-46 chance of attending college in 1972, a 1-in-13,342,000 chance of becoming one of the first black anchorwomen in history, and a 1-in-265,453,000 chance of becoming the most powerful person on television.

It was Denis Diderot who proclaimed that only passion; great passion could elevate the soul to great things.

Quincy Jones is the all-time most nominated Grammy artist, with a total of 79 nominations and 27 awards. However, Quincy grew up so impoverished that he and his brother would go down to the Ohio River in Kentucky to hunt rats. They would bring the dead rats' home, and their grandmother would fry them for dinner.

Not only was Walt Disney fired for not being creative, but he was also turned down over three hundred times before he received financing for his dream of building, The Happiest Place on Earth.

When Ray Kroc started the McDonald's franchise, he was fifty-two, had diabetes and crippling arthritis. He lost his gall bladder and most of his thyroid glands but was convinced that the best was yet to come. His wife was dissatisfied with her husband taking such a gamble so late in life. She didn't share his vision and thought that hamburgers were something that one made in the backyard. They later divorced, but Ray went on to realize his dreams, and McDonalds is one of the largest and most profitable franchises on the planet. Sometimes the people who start out on the journey with us will not be able to go all the way. You have to decide what the dream is worth and what price you are willing to pay.

Michael Dell was laughed and scoffed at when he spoke of his idea of selling computers over the internet. He was told, "Fool, you need a computer to get on the internet!"

"I never knew a guitar player worth a damn." Vernon Presley, to his young son Elvis, in 1954

"We don't believe that The Beatles will do anything in this market." Jay Livingstone, head of Capitol Records, in 1964.

Many people told Sam Walton that his idea of large discount stores in small towns was insane. Now Wal-Mart is the number one retailer in the world.

Colonel Sanders was rejected over one thousand times before he heard his first, 'Yes."

When Alexander Graham Bell invented the telephone, the corporate heads at Western Union remarked that such an invention was inherently of no value to them. President Rutherford B. Hayes declared that it was an interesting invention, but there is absolutely no practical use for it.

The point is, even if a major corporation and the President of the world's most significant Super Power do not believe in your dream, that does not make your idea a foolish one. Pursue your passion! I could write several books about all the great men and women who had to overcome insurmountable odds to achieve their dreams. It has become apparent by now that there is no such thing as an impossible dream. Overnight, the impossible might not become possible, but over time, the impossible will undoubtedly become possible. You might not be able to add more years to your life, but if you desire to add more life to your years, then, by all means, pursue your passion. The great men and women in history weren't great when they got started; they got started to be great. Understand that you came here to be legendary, not secondary, so step out of your comfort zone and into your greatness. Pursue your passion.

I know that the next logical question will be, "Well, what if I don't know what my passion is?" In my Pursue Your Passion Workshop, there are various exercises that the participant goes through to uncover their passion; one of them is going through the process of elimination to clear the mental clutter. If you know what your passion is not, be sure that you're not engaged in that activity trying to make a living. It will never work. You're only gathering nails for your coffin. Refuse to stay in a dead-end job or relationship because you're seeking security. Security comes from within, never without.

Be willing to walk by faith and not by sight; trust the God within you. Understand that the little voice that keeps on ministering to your heart was not placed there to torment you; it was placed there to spur you on towards your dreams. Let's start by eliminating the stuff that is not your passion that you're engaged in, and then let's remove the idea that there are things that you enjoy doing, but you do not know how to make a living doing these things so therefore they cannot be considered a viable passion.

Also, pay attention to what upsets you, what gnaws away at your soul. The things that resonate with us on an emotional level are usually the things that were placed there for us to either solve or improve. Dr. King was deeply concerned about injustice, equal rights, and humanity. These were the things that kept him up at night, and these were the areas that he set out to impact.

That crazy idea that you're passionate about is your divine assignment. It is what you signed up for, the very reason you're here, and the same reason this book has found you. Never dismiss your ideas as crazy or unreasonable. Are they any more irrational than the Pet Rock, which sold millions? Are they any more unreasonable than Hula Hoops or the Slinky? What about difficulty? Is your idea any more difficult than splitting the atom or placing a man on the moon? Only those who attempt the ridiculous will ever achieve the spectacular, so you can either make excuses, or you can make a difference, but you certainly cannot make both. Go to your destiny and make a difference; the world is counting on you. Depending on the choices that you make, you'll either live your dreams, or you will live your excuse.

You Deserve Better:

Is has been estimated that there are over 50 trillion cells in the human body,

That is trillion with a, 'T.'

And it has been further proven that each of those cells

Has within it, consciousness.

In other words, intelligence.

Intelligence that our most supercalifragilisticexpialidocious

Awesome computer cannot duplicate.

I said cannot duplicate.

Now please allow me to put this into perspective.

Because we've designed a computer,

Where in a remote office in Virginia sits a man.

And this man can pilot an unmanned vehicle in Afghanistan,

And out of a population of millions, target one individual.

One individual who does not look like him,

Does not dress like him, does not pray like him,

And not believe like him.

And with one decision he can eradicate that man

With such precision in the fields of Afghanistan,

That the body would be dead before it hits the ground.

And he can leave his office with enough time to be back home with no strife,

To sit and watch the current episode of Scandal with his wife.

Because Olivia Pope has never been this dope,

And as long as it's not your scandal that's being brought to light

Or you and your spouse had a fight,

Then you'll pretty much sleep all right tonight.

Yet that billion-dollar supercomputer

And that multi-million-dollar drone is garbage

Compared to the intelligence found in one of your cells,

And you have over fifty trillion of those cells in your body.

So my question is, "Is this it?"

As intelligent a Being as you are, the life that you are living,

Is that the best life that you can design for yourself?

IS THIS IT?

Is this the best that we can do?

And if we should be honest with ourselves

Then the answer would be a resounding,

'No!' to just about everything that we do.

So my question is, "What's stopping you?"

What's stopping you from no longer getting up at the crack of dawn

To hurry up and get dressed just to sit in bumper to bumper traffic,

To get to a job that is stressing you,

To serve a boss who doesn't appreciate you,

Who sees no value in you?

And forget that your stomach is trying to get you out of your seat

But this boss assigns you the time of day that you are allowed to eat.

And even though you're a grown adult who doesn't believe in games,

Nor do you indulge in tricks

But if you're out for more than two days, then you better prove that you were sick.

Now you're deep in debt, so you're praying, "Lord have mercy."

Because you fought adversity in New Jersey,

To graduate that prestigious University.

And a degree called a Masters is what they gave

Because you bought into the idea that the road to the American Dream,

This degree will pave.

But here you are ten years later, with a Masters, and you're still a slave.

And every day your joy is getting just a little bit harder to summon,

Because you know ain't no proclamation coming.

And you can feel breathing down your neck, the breath of fear

Because this dream is now beginning

To look like the American nightmare.

And if you think about climbing that corporate ladder,

My brother, don't even bother.

Not the way they pit you against each other.

Your coworker? Oh, you're going to have to jerk her,

She's a necessary adversary smiling in your face,

And sometimes you have to skin a few cats

For a piece of cheese in this rat race.

But thank God for saving grace,

Today you're putting in your request six months in advance,

Without leaving your assigned station

Looking forward to that one week off to take the family on vacation.

But keeping up with the bills doesn't afford you the sensation

Of traveling across this great nation.

So just like last year, once again, you're doing a STAYcation.

You're staying at home, damn near depressed,

But no time to think about that; got get back to your desk,

Because they keep you pressed, health deteriorating from the stress

But oh yes, TGIF.

So you rush to your car,

Hoping to do Happy Hour at the bar.

But instead, you're back to doing the bumper to bumper thing my dear,

And just like that traffic, your life is going nowhere.

And you long for all the beauty of life to be showered,

If only you could be a part of a network that's empowered.

And if you want to be something that you've never been

Then today you're going to have to do something that you've never done.

So how long are you going to remain cautious to the point of being nauseous?

What will it take for you to get off the hamster wheel of this nation?

What will it take for you to transcend Maslow's hierarchy of needs

From security to self-actualization?

You are by no means powerless,

So I am asking you not just to sit there and fret.

How long are you going to tiptoe through life,

Hoping to arrive safely at death?

You were created by Divine Source and infinite intelligence it gave,

Freedom is your birthright from the cradle to the grave.

So believe me when I tell you that

YOU DID NOT COME HERE TO BE NO SLAVE!

No slave to no job.

No slave to no bills.

No slave to no student loans.

No slave to no credit score.

THAT IS NOT WHAT YOU WERE CREATED FOR.

There is someone out there who is coming from

A much darker place than you have ever seen

And believe me when I tell you that today, she's living your dreams.

So it doesn't matter who you are and what you do

I'm saying that dream in your heart; it's possible for you.

So look at your gifts and begin to take stock

Because in order to make this leap,

You're not only going to have to think,

You're going to have to act outside of the box.

But you're thinking; if you don't have a job, then you're done,

I'm asking you, please, stop beating that drum.

In today's economy, you don't need a job; you need an income.

And Life will grind you to a pulp if you let her

But she will yield to your desires if with conviction you tell her,

That I deserve better!

So send this life of mediocrity and compromise back to the kitchen,

I am now creating from a perspective that is much broader

This nonsense is just not what I ordered.

And I know as pathetic as it sounds,

Your ego would rather me not say this,

But tiptoe around the issue and have you continue to live in fear

However, it is your best thinking that has brought you here.

So if there are some new skills that you need to acquire

Then by God, go ahead and get 'em

If there are some books that you need to read

Then listen when someone else suggests 'em

And if someone has created some training on the internet,

Then God bless 'em

And if you have to step outside of your comfort zone,

Then you better start stepping,

Be open to the lessons,

Be willing to look at opportunities with new eyes

And stop blocking your blessings.

Because this is what I know to be true,

The dream that is possible for me is also possible for you.

So I am asking you…

I am asking you today to commit to the life that you've always adored

I am asking you today to walk away from mediocrity and slam the door

I am asking you today to step out

On the playing field of life with the intention to score

And it is not over until you walk away with your dreams;

No, not a moment before.

So basically, I'm asking you today to decide to be a slave no more.

CHAPTER 6

THE COURAGE TO PERSIST

"I will persist until I succeed."
Og Mandino

Persistence is a mandatory ingredient in the recipe for success. The interesting thing about life is that everything has a price. The price for your dreams must be paid in full and in advance before the dream can be realized. Most people are aware of this, even if it's just on a cellular level. The problem lies in the fact that they are usually willing to pay *a* price for their dreams and ideals, but unfortunately, they fall short of paying ***the*** price.

It's very similar to a man dying of thirst and desperately needing a drink of water. He stumbles onto a water vending machine, dispensing that lifesaving drink which he urgently needs. The price of the water is not posted on the machine, just two slots; one for coins and one for bills. He searches his pockets and comes up with three quarters, which he eagerly deposits into the machine. Nothing happens. He digs a little deeper and discovers that he had a dime that he wasn't aware of, so he makes another deposit. The machine makes a churning noise, but still, no water. He frantically searches all his other pockets and finds only six pennies. In a frenzied state, he nervously deposits each penny; lights started blinking on the machine but still, no water. Realizing that he has searched all his pockets and had given the machine everything that he thought he had, he begins to panic. He proceeds to verbally and physically assault the machine in a desperate effort to get the water. After all, he gave the stupid machine everything that he had, only to receive nothing in return. In a futile attempt to beat the machine into submission, he loses all his strength and energy, and he later dies of thirst, frustration, and exhaustion.

A few days later, a woman comes along and begins depositing coins into the machine. The machine gladly gives up the bottle of water, which she immediately enjoys. A stranger curiously inquires, "How much does that water cost?"

"Oh, it's a dollar!"

Meanwhile, back at the morgue, the undertaker discovers that our friend who died of thirst and frustration had one hundred and twenty dollars tucked away in his boots. Aparrently he was afraid of being robbed, so he hid his valuables in his boots and forgot about it. If only he had dug a little deeper.

The fact that the price for the water isn't conspicuously posted on the vending machine is what scares the bejeezus out of most people. If they knew the exact cost of their dream, they could decide if they were willing to make such a sacrifice. Unfortunately, life is a tad more complicated. When the man began depositing coins in the machine, the machine started lighting up and making churning noises. It was apparent that there was some activity going on, but that was of no relevance to the man because it was not the activity that he was seeking.

As we move towards our dreams, a lot of things are taking place in the unseen. Things that are not apparent to the naked eye. That's why we are instructed to walk by faith and not by sight. The Law of Attraction is always pulling our dominant thoughts and desires towards us, but until those thoughts manifest and are made flesh, it is challenging to gauge exactly how close we are. Faith allows us to walk confidently in the direction of our goals. With sufficient faith, we won't need to see any evidence of our desired results. Our faith becomes evidence. "Faith is the substance of things hoped for, the evidence of things not seen."

The man attempting to purchase the water became filled with fear once he wasn't given any evidence that the water would be forthcoming. Fear is the opposite of faith. In fact, fear is faith that it won't work out. According to the Law of Attraction, one of two things will manifest in your life. You will live your fears, or you will live your faith. Feed your faith, and your fears will starve to death. It is challenging to persist if you don't believe that things will get better. Nothing kills a dream faster than a series of discouragements. So even when things are looking the darkest, continue to feed your faith that you are destined to have your dream. Longfellow reminds us that, "The heights by great men, reached and kept were not attained by sudden flight. But they, while their companions slept, were toiling upwards during the night."

If you want to be something that you've never been, you have to do something that you've never done. In other words, if we want our dreams, we have to look in places that we've never looked before. The man was accustomed to looking in his pockets for money but forgot that money could be kept in his boots. After all, he placed the money there because he was fearful that he might get robbed. He kept his most prized possession so profoundly hidden that not even he could find it. Once he searched his pockets, he believed that he had exhausted all of his funds and resources. Not true!

More often than not, when we believe that we've given our all, there is usually a lot more inside of us if we just dig a litter deeper. He believed that his all was ninety-one cents when in fact, it was more than one hundred and twenty times that amount.

I've read of a woman who weighed only one hundred and eleven pounds, yet she lifted a car weighing over a ton, off her son, who was in an accident. We've read of people lost in the mountains and surviving freezing temperatures for days with little or no resources. The human spirit is unstoppable, but first, we must resolve not to be stopped.

The dying man uncovered ninety-one cents from his consciousness. All he needed was nine cents more. Maybe if he knew that all he needed was nine cents, he would've found a way to persevere. Being that he had no idea what the price of the water was, he assumed that it was out of his reach. Very often, we give up when our dreams are within our grasp. We turn away and walk off the field of life when we're on the one-yard line, a yard away from the end zone. Sometimes we consume a great deal of energy, focusing on how far we have to go. If we instead shift our focus to how far we have traveled, we would find the strength to take the next step. In the words of Dr. Wayne Dyer, "When we change the way that we look at things (situations) the things (situations) we look at, change."

When I left my job as a furniture salesman and decided that I wanted to be a full-time poet, I knew there was a price to pay, however, I wasn't aware of the exact cost. Nor was I aware that pursuing my passion for poetry would evolve into me being a speaker, trainer, and author; however, I was earnest in my resolve never to return to the job market. I was committed to the idea that I could figure out how to make this passion work for me.

I was clueless about what such a commitment would cost; the only thing I knew with absolute certainty was that I would never go back to working for someone. Going back was not an option; my attitude was simple: No retreat, no surrender. I thought it would take me a year or two (and maybe a little discomfort) to be able to make a living from my art. Well, it took my lights being shut off for nonpayment. It took my phone being disconnected. It took having ice for breakfast and water for dinner. It took being evicted from my apartment and sleeping in my car or sometimes on a friend's couch. It took family members interpreting my refusal to get a job as a lack of ambition and irresponsibility. It took borrowing money and not being able to repay the loan for years. It took having my car repossessed. It took my son being suspended from school because I could not pay the tuition. It took my name being dragged through the mud by people who were threatened by my resolve. It took my credit score sliding from 780 to somewhere around 500. It took a woman walking out of my life with the parting words, "If you were going to make it, you would've made it by now." In short, it took well over a decade!

The time that it took was irrelevant. What was relevant was that I was willing to sacrifice who I was for who I could become. I understood the process. I realized that if you're pregnant with purpose and passion, you have to go through labor pains before you can give birth.

Most women who have complications during pregnancy lose the baby within the first few months or in the early stages of pregnancy. As time goes by, the fetus grows, gets more robust and has a much better chance of surviving. The mother also becomes more emotionally attached to the child and will fight with every ounce of willpower, every cell of her being, to keep that baby alive.

The same is true for a dream. Most dreams die in the early stages. The pregnant partner cannot envision how she will support this baby. So the dream is quickly and quietly aborted and only spoken of in shame and inaudible whispers. But once you begin to work with your dreams for a few trimesters, that dream takes on a life of its own and becomes impossible to abort. Once you get off the milk of mediocrity and start feeding your mind the diet of determination, the discipline of daily prenatal care, that baby will develop its heartbeat. You now become nauseated by the unnecessary as your body rejects everything that is not conducive to the well-being of your dream. You move away from energy drainers because your fetus becomes fatigued in the presence of foolishness. You swallow large doses of faith, which becomes your Folic Acid and release fear as if it were fiber. Once you've been working with your dream and envisioning the result, the dream begins to grow and kick in your stomach. It gnaws at your guts; it nibbles at your nerves, and it sits on your bladder and keeps you up at night. It reminds you that I am here, and I am alive. You can feel it stretching in your belly, just waiting to be birthed. As you work with the dream, you'll begin to get back pains, and your belly button will swell. Your breasts will become enlarged because they're engorged with enthusiasm. You will tell all the people who believe that you're too young to have this dream, or that you need to be married, or complete your education first, that they don't have to believe in your dreams. You laid with your Divine Source, became pregnant by Immaculate Conception, and now you're in labor and looking forward to giving birth to something spectacular.

The thing that kept me going through all the labor pains and struggles was the information that I kept feeding my mind. Romans 12 v 2 reads: And be not conformed to this world, but be ye transformed by a renewing of your mind. So I refused to be conformed to the thinking of this world. The thought that the odds are against me, or that it is impossible to make it on your own or that my color played a role in what was possible for me in America. Instead, I renewed my mind by reading all the books of people who had to endure more, far more than I did, and still managed to make it. I read the narratives of Fredrick Douglas. I read the autobiography of Quincy Jones, Johnnie Cochran, Walt Disney, Oprah Winfrey, Ray Kroc, and Fred Smith. I listened to tapes that sold me on my greatness; Les Brown, Earl Nightingale, Napoleon Hill, Og Mandino, Anthony Robbins, Jim Rohn, Dr. Bruce Lipton, and numerous others. Whenever the chips were down, I thought, "If Quincy Jones can eat a damn rat for dinner and went on to win all those Grammies, I can certainly sleep in my car and go on to write a best seller!"

I made sure that every paragraph of everything that I read was packed with spiritual protein. As long as I was reading of other people who overcame tremendous odds, my odds didn't seem so long after all. As long as I lifted my eyes to the hills, I was able to walk on water, but as soon as I focused on the thunder and lightning, just like Peter in the Bible, I began to sink.

When the storms of life show up (and they will), understand that the storm is doing what it is supposed to do. The gale-force winds of discouragement, the thunderous blows of trouble, the rain of betrayal, the flashfloods of fever and false friends, the storm surge of sickness, the tropical depressions, and disappointments, are all a part of the checks and balances which are meant to allow only those who are willing to persist into the promised land. Let the storm do what it does; your job is to do what you do, and that is to persist.

Believe in your dream so strongly that you will continue to move forward and trust your heart, even though your reality has yet to show any signs of the manifestation of that dream. Your job is to keep on rowing through the storm. Be confident in the crisis, be calm in the face of chaos because the truth of the matter is; this too shall pass. Trouble did not come to stay; it came to pass. Be steadfast in your action, like a seasoned boxer, stick and move, stick, and move.

Sometimes you may need to row faster to escape the storm. Rowing more quickly means increasing your activities, be it rising earlier and making more phone calls, jogging one more lap, seeing one more client, or asking one more person for help. Sometimes rowing faster is not the solution. There are times when it makes more sense to wait out the storm. Get away for the weekend, take a walk on the beach, do something to recharge your spirit, or just simply, "Be still and know that I AM God!"

"I've missed more than 9,000 shots in my career. I've lost almost 300 games. Twenty-six times, I've been trusted to take the game-winning shot and missed. I've failed over and over and over again in my life. And that is why I succeed." -Michael Jordan

When he was 22, he failed in business, at the age of 23, he ran for the legislature and lost. When he was 24, he failed in business again. The following year he was elected to the legislature; however, the very next year tragedy struck, his sweetheart died. At the age of 27, he had a nervous breakdown. Within two years, he was defeated for the post of Speaker of the House in the State Legislature. When he was 31, he was defeated as Elector. At the age of 34, he ran for Congress and lost. When he was 37, he ran for Congress and finally won. Two years later, he ran again and lost his seat in Congress. At the age of 46, he ran for the U.S. Senate and lost. The following year he ran for Vice President and lost that, too. He ran for the Senate again, and once again, he lost. Finally, at the age of 51, he was elected President of the United States. Who was this perpetual loser? Abraham Lincoln.

Twenty-three publishers rejected Dr. Suess' first children's book. The twenty-fourth sold six million copies. John H. Johnson, the man who founded Jet and Ebony magazine, faced countless rejections, unbelievable discrimination, and almost impossible odds before he was able to generate enough support to keep his magazines alive. I believed that these men kept their focus on their ultimate destination. They didn't dwell on the past defeats and the previous rejections. They pressed on towards their unfolding destiny, forgetting those things which are behind and reaching forth unto those things which are before. Ralph Waldo Emerson said, "Men succeed when they realize that their failures are the preparation for their victories."

Where the attention goes, the energy flows. If you want something to grow in your life, give it your attention. If you want a better relationship with your spouse, give the relationship more attention, and it will flourish, this is a simple law that we've all misused at one point or another, and therefore inadvertently used it to dig our graves. If we start placing our attention on all that is going wrong in our lives, then the wrong things will grow and multiply in our lives. The trick to life is being able to manage where you place your attention. When all hell breaks loose around you, if you can manage to keep your eyes focused on your highest ideals, lifted onto the hills, then you will begin to uncover unexpected ways out of your situation. You will find yourself navigating the winds of change.

Always tell yourself, "I can survive this. I win regardless." When things go wrong, don't go with them. Don't give your so-called failures your focus. Do not marinate in your misery; keep on moving. That movement will create momentum, and that momentum can move mountains. Amid my struggles, I found myself yelling at life, "Is this it? A Sickle Cell crisis? Homelessness? Bad credit? When are you going to get it? I can't be stopped; I am never turning back, I don't care what you hit me with, I am not leaving without my dreams." You start doing that, and ordinary folks will start calling you crazy, and when you begin appearing crazy to ordinary folks, that's when you know that you're well on your way to a breakthrough.

Have you ever asked someone what do they want out of life? The first thing that they usually say is, "Well, I know what I don't want." And often, that is precisely what they attract. They have unconsciously placed their attention on what they don't want, and by the Laws of Attraction, that is precisely what they receive. Always place your attention on what you want to see in your life, not on what you don't want. Discipline your mind to dwell on only what you want. If an unwanted thought enters your mind, replace it with a thought of desire that you want to see manifest. You must be able to hold the vision. Where there is no vision, the people perish. If that statement is true, then the converse must also hold true. Where there is vision, the people prosper, because hope in the future translates to power in the present. Below is a post that I shared on my blog almost a decade ago, but the concept still rings true.

To manifest the best, there are three things that we need to be mindful of: Our Intention, our Attention, and the last is No Tension (our level of stress). What I want to focus on is attention and the reason it is so important. Teachers, parents, and other authoritarians would insist that we "Pay attention." They never said, "give" your attention to something. They said for you to "pay" attention because attention always costs something.

Remember your last relationship, the one that didn't work out? Remember when you first met and started dating. The person that you cared about not only received all of your attention but also the attention that they received was undivided. You would pick up the phone on the first ring if they were calling. If you were on another call when their call came through, you would get rid of the other person on the line. And God forbid, you missed their call, you'd call back immediately. You went to the movies, held hands, and then you'd be on the phone at the end of the night engaged in nonsensical conversation just to show them that they've captured your attention. When the relationship began to fade, one of the first things that went out the door was your attention. Now when the phone rings, you let it go to voicemail. Instead of calling you, send a text. Before you would call back immediately when you missed their calls, now several hours (even days) passed before you gave your attention to the matter. Eventually, the relationship dies.

Attention is like sunlight, whatever you place in its path, it causes to grow, bloom and flourish. If there is anything in your life that you want to see flourish and prosper, simply give it more attention. If you want a raise at your job, be more attentive to the needs of your employer. Spend time considering how to reduce the stress level on the job, how to improve customer relations etc. If it is better health that you desire, focus your attention on the food that you're putting in your body, give more attention to exercising and getting the proper amount of rest.

Unfortunately, it would appear that most Americans are almost incapable of focused attention. We've ALLOWED our attention to be manipulated. Concentrated attention is the source of our power, yet we willingly give it away only to complain that we feel so powerless. Ironic, isn't it? Not so long ago, the primary topic on television was healthcare. Every blog, every Facebook update, and Twitter conversation included the same rhetoric that the public was being spoon-fed. For some strange reason, the majority of Americans seemed to be obsessed with healthcare. We then moved on to Chris Brown and Rihanna, and once again, America went down the path that was paved for them. Soon we became bored with the young couple, so we were given the President and his Nobel Peace Prize, and then we were given Tiger Woods and his domestic affairs. After we became bored with those issues, we were told to focus on who Nicki Minaj is dating, why LeBron left Miami, or the fact that Oprah gained an extra pound over the Thanksgiving holidays.

Whatever the media puts on the front page, that's what we give our attention, and it is impossible to give your "undivided" attention to more than one thing at a time. With your attention being spread among all of these compelling stories, the most important things aren't getting your undivided attention. Before you know it, the years go by, and you haven't achieved your goals because they became secondary. You have given more time and attention to Tiger than your priorities. So in two years, you will be able to recall everything that went down in Tiger's marriage, but you will not be able to remember how the time in your life was invested.

Scattering your attention, allowing yourself to be seduced by headlines that are not conducive to your goals, can never lead you to your desired destination. Get a journal, start a journal, and start giving attention to outlining your goals. They should be the last thing you think about when you go to bed and the first thing on your mind when you wake up. Your attention is the source of your power. FOCUS and MANIFEST.

Renewing your mind is only the beginning of the process. It is the fuel that will keep you in the fight, but to win, you must keep on punching. You can listen to all the motivational tapes there are, chant all the mantras from the mystics of the East, quote all the scriptures from the holy books, and meditate on the profundity of life. But if you do not start punching in this ring of life, you will be knocked down and knocked out. It is not enough to want to win; you must expect to win.

Expectation shows up in preparation. Success boils down to how you spend your time. If you want to know where a person is going in life, observe how they spend their downtime. The reason it is called downtime is that this is usually the time when we are engaged in activities that keep us from moving up. The person who expects success prepares for success.

It is challenging to persist if we believe that we're chasing an impossible dream. That's why reading the stories of people who had to overcome impossible odds is so important. This very act will help to redefine your ideas of what is possible. It prepares the mind for the great things which are to unfold. The reason passion is so important is because it is almost impossible to persist if you're not passionate about the idea that you're pursuing. If it's not your passion, at the first sign of trouble, you will retreat. You will abandon your dream and eventually return to the safety and familiarity of your comfort zone.

Spend your time preparing to enter your promise land. Abraham Lincoln said, "If I had eight hours to cut down a tree, I would spend six sharpening my axe."

As you think about your dreams and ideals, as you spend more time preparing for it, you begin to draw it towards you. You begin to attract the thing that you prepare for. We've seen how this works against us all the time. We've seen people enter relationships in a very guarded manner, thinking that in the event the relationship doesn't work, they won't be hurt too badly. Eventually, the relationship ends in a disaster, and they mumble to themselves, "I knew it wouldn't work." But the fact of the matter is, they were preparing for a doomed relationship, and that's what life delivered.

Prepare by doing something daily that will move you closer to your dreams. When I started pursuing my dreams of being a spoken word artist (poet), I began by committing my poetry to memory. That gave me the ability to perform my poetry, emotionally charging each word, by punctuating them with my body language, as opposed to merely reading from the page. Because my words were more emotionally impacting, I quickly developed a fan base, and because I had a fan base, promoters would book me for shows that would pay anywhere from $20 to $50 for the night. It wasn't a lot of money, but it was enough to help me survive one more day while I worked on the dream.

Discipline is the bridge that will get you over the troubled waters that are between you and your dream. It has been said that the man who lives without discipline will eventually die without dignity. Jim Rohn says, "Rest assured that in life, you will suffer from one of two pains. You will bear the pain of discipline, or you must bear the pain of regret. The pain of discipline weighs an ounce; the pain of regret weighs a ton."

Develop the daily discipline to work on being a little better than you were before. How do you develop this discipline? Emotionally visualize the outcome that you want, see your success in your mind's eye. Days (sometimes weeks) before I delivered a speech, I would spend time visualizing in my mind a very receptive audience, an audience walking away from the speech being fired up and inspired. I would 'see' myself on stage; I would observe my body language and the audience's reaction. I would 'feel' the heat from the spotlights that were focused on me. In short, I would 'see' myself giving a very successful speech.

Once I was finished with that meditation, I would be so fired up that I wanted to do everything in my power to make that vision a reality. So naturally, I would immediately work on my material, commit more stories, analogies, quotes, and statistics to memory. The discipline to keep my tools sharp became a habit because the picture in my mind was so clearly defined. Discipline is the ability to do what you're supposed to do, whether you feel like it or not. Develop the habit of doing the things that failures refuse to do. Spend your days sharpening your axe, perfecting your craft, and you will become undeniable. Small differences in ability lead to a tremendous difference in results.

A racehorse that wins by a nose wins ten times the prize money than the horse that comes in second. Yet he is not ten times better than the horse he beats; he's not even twice as fast. He is only faster by a nose. Little things make a big difference. The difference between a gold and a silver medal is 1/1000th of a second.

After 12 grueling rounds of boxing, 36 minutes of exchanging vicious blows, a boxing match usually comes down to one or two points. Develop discipline so that you can be a little bit better. After all the fouls, the timeouts, the planning, the training, the strategy, a basketball game usually comes down to one or two baskets. Develop the discipline so that you can be a little bit better. After all the pain, the yards, the flags, the infractions, the injury, a football game usually boils down to one or two plays. Be a little bit better.

The most talented are often overtaken by the most dedicated. The future must be purchased with the present, so be willing today to do the things that others won't do, so tomorrow, you can have the things others won't have.

If you are working the typical forty hours per week, discipline yourself to spend at least one hour per day working on your dreams. If you can commit eight hours per day building someone else's dream, you must dedicate at least one hour per day to yours. In, Lead

The Field, Earl Nightingale explains that if you total the hours in a year and then subtract the sleeping hours, assuming that you sleep eight hours every night, you'll find that you have about 5,840 waking hours of which 2,000 are spent on the job.

So this leaves about 3,840 discretionary hours when you're neither sleeping nor working. If you took just one hour per day for five days per week and worked on your dreams, this one action alone will accelerate your success tremendously. In that hour, work on moving closer to your desired destination, work on getting the necessary information that will take you to your promised land, then act on that information. Ignorance re-enforces fear, so the more you learn about your dreams, the more courage you'll develop to move towards your ideals. Take a completely blank sheet of paper and write down as many ideas as you can to improve your lot.

Twenty ideas per day are the equivalent of one hundred ideas per week. One hour per day/five days per week equates to 260 hours per year and still leaves you with over 3,500 hours of free time. This means that you'll be thinking about your goals and ways to improve your life for six and a half, full working weeks per year. Six and a half, 40 hour weeks, devoted to working and planning. Small differences lead to tremendous results. I do realize that the realities of life seldom allow us to fit our schedule into a perfect mathematical formula.

The point that I'm making is that if we took one hour per day, we would still have plenty of time left. I would call my older sister, and it would be days before she returned my call. She always apologized and told me that she was very busy. I never bought her excuses because I knew that no one is that busy; I'm just not a priority. If her son's teacher called her during the school day, she would either pick up or return the call immediately because such a call would be viewed as a priority in her mind. My point is, we will always make time for what is important to us.

Be willing to fight for your dreams, even if you end up fighting alone. Earlier, we discussed the fact that most people will not believe in your dreams. It would be nice to have folks stand your ground with you, but it's not necessary. As long as you believe in your vision and continue to move forward, you will eventually attract the people who can propel you along your path. Sometimes it is challenging for members of our family to see our greatness because they're usually more familiar with our fears and insecurities, so it becomes almost impossible for them to look beyond your fears and see your dreams. A hero is very seldom celebrated in his hometown because of the same issue of familiarity. A lot of times, you will have to go outside of your family (your comfort zone) to realize your greatness. I've heard it said that your friends are God's way of apologizing for your family, and unfortunately, sometimes that cliché rings true.

Between you and your dream, there is a chasm called trouble. Whenever trouble enters the room, false friends usually exit the room. That's when you must strengthen your resolve. Write your goals down, and review them daily, lie in bed at night and visualize the success that you're seeking. Experience that state with all the emotions that you can muster. An easy way to conjure the emotional state of your dreams being fulfilled is by questioning yourself. Let's assume that your goal is to sing the national anthem at halftime during the Super Bowl. Go someplace quiet and just relax, close your eyes and see yourself at the Super Bowl singing. Then ask yourself, "How does that feel?" "What would it feel like if I had my dream?" Then spend as much time in that feeling as possible. Forget about 'how' you're going to make the dream happen for now;

just focus on the feeling of the wish being fulfilled. Neville Goddard states that a presumption, though false if persisted in, will harden into facts.

So allow your mind to drift and experience the emotions. See the crowd rising to their feet for the singing of the anthem. Keep that picture in your mind's eye, and your RAS will begin to pull that image towards you and you towards it. I have accomplished more in my life with this process than any other. Hold the vision until it becomes real in your mind, then release it. Let it dissolve from your mind. Go about your day in confidence, knowing that thy will has been accomplished. When you believe it, you will see it.

Revisiting our friend and the water vending machine, after exhausting his resources and not appearing to be any closer to his goal, he became bitter. He began cursing and physically abusing the machine. Once we become discouraged, we tend to despise the thing that once held our affection. I've known folks who were married for six years, got divorced, and then complained that their spouse was, "No good." If they were no good, you would've never married them in the first place. They had to have some good in them. Never curse anything that you want, whatever you curse will come back and curse you. Bless everything, and you will be blessed by everything. Thoughts are boomerangs, and they always return home, so get in the habit of blessing everyone, everything, and every situation.

Dr. Martin Luther King Jr. and Mahatma Gandhi would not have been able to overcome an oppressive government by attacking the government with the same negative energy that the government showed them. They had to shine Light into the darkness. Had they used force, it would've been met by the superior forces of the government. They melted the cold darkness of their oppressors' consciousness with the warmth of their Light. The same principle holds true for any relationship; resistance must be met with nonresistance. There is no need to beat the machine into submission, just keep applying coins with the knowledge that life will yield to you. You cannot lose. Press on because you were born to win, destined to be great. Believe that the best is on its way. Hope is one of the greatest gifts given to us by God. We endure the tough times only when we believe in the future.

Do you recall that in our water vending story, a woman came along a few days later and purchased a bottle of water? A stranger asked, "How much does the water cost?"

And she replied, "One dollar!"

The significant point here is that if the stranger ever needed water, he knew in advance what the price would be. The woman was his mentor; she instructed him on the price that he would have to pay to have water. We can save ourselves a lot of time, effort, and aggravation if we turn to mentors for help. The books that I read were my initial mentors. Still, when it was time to get serious about the speaking business, I went and signed up for a Speaker Training Seminar conducted by one of the top motivational speakers in the world, Mr. Les Brown himself.

I remember telling someone that I paid $5,000 for the training, and they exclaimed, "$5,000! That's crazy! The trainer must be making a killing."

They were focused on what the training cost, obviously missing the point that it's not what the book costs, it's what it costs if you don't read it. Not only did that $5,000 investment cut years off my learning curve as a speaker, but it allowed me to network with like-minded folks. People who wish to wallow in mediocrity will always object to the price of investing in themselves, yet they will seldom object to the cost of shoes or admission to a nightclub. They will never have time to read a book because that would take away from the countless hours that they need to spend in front of the television.

Jim Rohn once told me that investing in your job will make you a living, and that is fine. Investing in yourself will make you a fortune, and that is fantastic. Seek out mentors who will be your bridge over troubled waters and help you persist in the face of discouragement. If you didn't have what it takes, your particular dream would not have been given to you, so begin moving in the direction of your ideals.

When I was seventeen years old, I heard Les Brown close his speech with a poem that I've committed to memory and kept close to my heart during challenging times. The poem simply says, "If you want a thing bad enough to go out and fight for it, to work day and night for it, to give up your time, your peace and sleep for it... if all that you dream and scheme is about it, ...and life seems useless and worthless without it... if you gladly sweat for it and fret for it and plan for it and lose all your terror of the opposition for it. If you simply go after that thing that you want with all your capacity, strength and sagacity, faith hope and confidence, and stern pertinacity. If neither cold, poverty, famine, nor gout, sickness nor pain, of body and brain, can keep you away from the thing that you want, if dogged and grim you beseech and beset it, with the help of God, YOU WILL GET IT!"

Dealers of Deceit

The only difference between you

And the greatest being to ever walk among mankind

Are the thoughts that you allow to occupy your mind.

Because deep within there is a warrior who is far more intense

And he keeps fighting even when it doesn't seem to make sense.

His allies are Hope, Faith, Determination, and Confidence

And when he fights, eyes have never witnessed such diligence.

No low blows because homeboy got a conscience

But his one-two punch is equivalent to some serious turbulence,

Causing disturbance in fear's influence.

This unbeatable warrior goes by the name Persistence.

So you can choose your fears and make them dictate your deeds

Or you can boldly declare, 'I will persist until I succeed!'

I will persist until I succeed!

Keep throwing the ball, never consider the fumble,

Keep hammering away until the mountain crumbles.

Bang away at life until it yields you some respect

Keep fighting until you put your fears in check.

Keep kicking even when you believe that you can't go on

And if you're at the end of your rope, tie a knot and hold on.

Let the critics have their say

But today you're going to feel the fear and do it anyway.

Breathe life into your dreams, for they are only asleep

Your destiny is here for you to court

Roll away the stone to the tomb of doubt

And command, 'Lazarus come forth!'

Excerpt from the poem, "Dealers of Deceit."

Taken from my book "Answer The Call."

THE COURAGE TO PERSIST

CHAPTER 7

THE BEAUTY OF MONEY

> "Money doesn't make you happy.
> I now have $50 million but
> I was just as happy when I had $48 million."
> –Arnold Schwarzenegger

There are a lot of religious folks walking around with the idea that money is evil. I will attempt to rid you of that idea by the end of this chapter. However, if I am unsuccessful, and you still believe that money is evil, then please visit my website at www.kirknugent.com and feel free to donate your evil funds to me. I wouldn't want it to corrupt you; it certainly will not corrupt me.

With that said, understand that money is neither good nor bad; it is our relationship with money that becomes constructive or destructive. We've all heard the scriptures being misquoted, "Money is the root of all evil." The passage actually reads, "The love of money is the root of all evil."

Of course, the love of anything driven to an obsession leads to the mismanagement of deeds or evil. Whenever I inject this argument into a conversation, there is always some righteous soul there to challenge me, "Well, you can never love the Lord too much." Then they'll proceed to recite scriptures that they've zealously committed to memory.

Fine! If you want to use the Bible to debate points of view, one could argue that the Bible and all great spiritual writings teach that love is the ultimate answer. Thou shalt not kill is right there in the Ten Commandments, however, because of powerful men loving their Lord, more people have been murdered in the name of the Lord (religion) than all other wars combined. More wars have been fought, and more people have been burned, tortured, exiled, and ostracized because righteous men loved their Lord.

I have also discovered that if anything is eviler than the love of money, it is the lack of money. People tend to become very agitated, and their fuse becomes extremely short when they're under financial duress. More people get divorced over arguments concerning money than they do adultery. Seventy percent of all crimes committed in the United States are committed because of some scheme involving money. Whenever money is in short supply, evil tends to run rampant. I am not telling you to serve money; in fact, money should be your servant. It should bow to you and yield to your will because you serve a God of abundance, not one of lack. You were given dominion over all that is on this Earth, and money is included in those things which were meant to submit to your will. You are a child of the Divine, and you were born blessed, never cursed, so stop behaving like the ocean dying of thirst.

We are royal aristocrats, born heir to the throne, yet our actions are more like an emperor who chooses to panhandle. We're like the sun believing that it is a simple candle. Remember your divinity and govern yourself accordingly.

What is very seldom quoted is a scripture in Ecclesiastes 10:19, which reads, "A feast is made for laughter, and wine maketh merry, but money answereth all things." ALL THINGS? Now you tell me, what does that exclude? I don't believe that money is the path to all happiness, but I also don't think it is the root of all evil. If we examine Maslow's hierarchy of needs, we will find survival is placed at the bottom. Once we have enough money to take care of our basic needs, then we can begin to move up the chart to self-actualization. Having sufficient money allows us more freedom of choice.

So in today's society money gives you options. Without options, you're enslaved. It provides the opportunity to secure the service of the best doctors for an ailing loved one. It gives the possibilities of helping the poor and feeding the needy. I remember witnessing friends going through a severe financial crisis and not being able to help because I was in the same boat if not worse. If their credit was bad, mine had AIDS. There is nothing evil about wanting to help relieve some of the sufferings in the world. The idea of money being evil is ludicrous. If there were any logic in that idea, then one could suppose that all of the money that celebrities gave to fight malaria and AIDS in Africa is the work of the devil. Our beloved Oprah, with all of her charitable work, building houses for the homeless, improving education for young girls, and with a heart as big as the Mississippi itself, she must be spawned from Beelzebub, and be on a top-secret mission to kill the world with kindness.

Another poorly developed idea that the uninitiated enjoy spoon-feeding the masses with is the cliché that "money can't buy happiness." I'm sure that in their logical minds, they have deduced that such a thing can be readily purchased with poverty. The philosophy of money being evil is ridiculous and doesn't even warrant a serious debate. After all, it is money that builds the churches, money that is used to purchase Bibles and books. Money creates missionaries that save people's lives, and money builds missiles that take people's lives. So keep it in perspective, there are certain things that money cannot buy, but in the areas in which money works, nothing can replace it. If you doubt the validity of that statement, here's a little litmus test. Call your mortgage lender or your landlord next month and tell them, "I don't have your money, but by God, I have a lot of love in my heart." Try doing that for ninety days; let me know what happens on the ninety-first. Be sure also to let me what soup kitchen you're calling from.

I believe that the idea of money being evil repels money from us. After all, who wants evil in their presence? If you asked most poor people if they wanted to be rich, they'd tell you that they want to be comfortable. There's another idea that will keep you broke. Comfortable people love their comfort zones, there's no growth in the comfort zone, and whatever isn't growing, is dying.

People who wish to be comfortable spend their time doing what's convenient; people who want to be financially independent invest their time in raising their financial IQ. I would always dig deeper and ask these comfort seekers, precisely what does comfortable look like? Describe if you will, precisely what would need to take place for you to be comfortable. They'll go on to say that they wished to be debt-free, be able to travel whenever and wherever they wanted to, put the kids through college without a struggle, and have money left over for a comfortable retirement. So I'd listen, then I'd ask, "Isn't that how rich people live?"

We need to create wealth, because we all need, "just in case" money. Just in case, Hurricane Katrina hits, and your flood insurance company tells you that even though your home is under ten feet of water, your damage was caused by the wind and, therefore, you're not covered. We need money just in case our parents or children need emergency surgery that your insurance doesn't cover. Just in case you're in the mood for a romantic getaway. Just in case, you decide that the job you've been on for the past decade no longer fulfills you.

Most people, whether they admit it or not, really want to be rich. No one wants to struggle financially, and even the most spiritual among us have very physical bills to attend to at the end of the month. With that said, let's speak about moving from financial embarrassment to financial independence.

Money is no different from anything else in our lives. Our state of mind will always determine our state of affairs. Before you can hold and keep money, it is imperative that you develop a consciousness mindset that attracts money. Money runs for cover in the face of fear; money never stays with the weak or the timid. Money flees from those who want a free lunch or something for nothing. Most people who win the state lottery are broke within five years. Money, like time, must never be squandered; it must be invested.

Never claim poverty and lack into your life. Never speak of what you cannot afford, but always speak in terms of prosperity. You will see that the principles that I speak of remain consistent throughout this book. The idea is to get your mind saturated with the thought that you were given dominion over everything, and that domination starts with your thoughts. Remember the principles that we've discussed in the earlier chapters. People who are asking to be comfortable, are not being specific and, therefore, they will miss their mark.

Les Brown always instructs his audience, "Shoot for the moon because even if you miss, you'll land among the stars." But if you're only shooting to be comfortable, if you miss, you might just end up on a government subsidy.

If wealth is what you seek, then claim it. Don't be shy about it; don't call it something that it's not. Just have the courage to start moving in that direction. It is evident that a job was not created to make you wealthy. The purpose of a job is to generate steady money to pay steady bills. To create wealth, you must renew your mindset; you must move from the thinking of a slave (employee) to the mentality of a master. Saturate your mind with the idea that you intend to create abundance in every area of your life. Some of the best books that I've read when it comes to increasing my financial IQ are the Rich Dad, Poor Dad series by Robert T. Kiyosaki. Invest in your financial education because financial ignorance is far more expensive than you can imagine.

Money should be your slave, and you should be its master. The paradox of this idea is that first, you might have to work like a slave to become a master. Look for ways of creating multiple streams of income. Think of this as having more than one burner on a stove. If you only have one burner, and the fire goes out under that burner, you could starve. But if you're cooking with two or more burners, you will never starve.

One of the reasons why it is so difficult to attain financial independence while working a nine to five is because you're trading your time for money. This is one of the worst ways to earn a living, there are only so many hours in the day, so ultimately there is a ceiling on what you're capable of earning. Besides, if you have to work twenty-four hours per day to earn a living, then you won't have any time to enjoy the fruits of your labor.

Most of us go to work and trade our moments for money. We sell ourselves to a company for so many hours of work, in return for a predetermined sum of money. The sad variable in this equation is what we do with the money when we finally get it in our hands. Usually, it all goes to pay bills and to maintain our standard of living, but very little is left for saving or investing. If we trade our time for money, then waste the money that we've sold our time for, we could very well be wasting our lives. To fully experience the joys of life, we must throw off all the shackles that enslave us. Debt is one such shackle that has kept the typical family chained in servitude to some financial institution or another.

Bear in mind that in any jungle, there are always predators. In the financial wilderness, there are predators that are systematically investing in our dysfunction. If you have decent credit and a financial institution can count on you to max out your credit cards at eighteen to twenty-one percent interest, then right now, you're one of the best investment vehicles on the planet. You're better than the stock market. You're better than mutual funds; you're better than the savings bonds. If you're in debt, your primary goal should be to get out of debt. Don't place another item on that charge card until you've paid it off, and if at all possible, once you've paid it off, don't charge anything else on there unless it's a genuine emergency. Seldom, if at all, can that new pair of shoes, or the power drill that is on sale, be considered an emergency expense. It makes no sense to purchase a pair of shoes that are on sale for 10% percent off and charge on a credit card accumulating twenty-one percent interest. Too many times, we buy our wants and beg for our needs.

That's why Robert Kiyosaki stresses the importance of financial IQ in his books. We need to know the actual difference between a liability and an asset. We need to understand how businesses work. If you only have one stream of income, then looking at a network marketing business is an excellent way to learn how big companies operate while earning some additional income. I call this "Pajama money." Money that you earn while you're asleep.

We must develop the habit of not living above our income. You can either cut back on your wants to fit your income as most people do, or you can increase your revenue to fit your wants comfortably. I prefer to supplement my income to meet my desires. A prerequisite for achieving this starts with careful planning, an exercise that the undisciplined have developed a disdain for doing. It has been said that wealthy people plan for generations; poor people tend to plan for Saturday nights.

If it is your goal to increase your wealth, then you must first educate yourself on how money works. Understand that we are living in the information age, and with a little effort, anything that we're trying to learn is readily available to us, so learn as much about the subject as you can. I am not saying that you need to be a savvy investor, you can always hire an expert for that, but you should at least know how long it would take your money to double if you placed it in an account at a fixed interest and left it there. If you educated yourself on the beauty of how time and compound interest can make anyone wealthy, you would have a better and brighter outlook.

Read Rich Dad, Poor Dad by Robert Kiyosaki, Secrets of the Millionaire Mind by T. Harv Eker and The Millionaire Fastlane by M.J. DeMarco. These books will open your mind up to a world of possibilities, plus they will serve to expand how you view money. It would not hurt to choose a life partner with a similar money psychology as yours. It creates terrible friction in a relationship if you're a saver, and your spouse is a spendthrift. It's okay to be philosophically promiscuous in certain areas of your relationships, but I've realized that when it comes to money, religion, and politics, it's best to be similarly yoked.

One of my favorite kinds of money is what I call, "pajama money" money that I earn while I'm sleeping. An example of "Pajama money" would be this book that you're reading. I invested the months that it took to write it, but I'll be paid for my work for years to come. While I'm in bed in Florida, someone will be purchasing the book in California or on the internet – and I'll get paid for that purchase.

When you're working a nine to five, the minute that you punch that time clock to leave for the day, your earning ability comes to a halt, definitely not a sound system for creating wealth. In fact, it is one of the most effective ways to stay broke in America. Passive residual income is, by definition, recurring revenue, but one that you are not working for. A great example of this would be to own a building with tenants. Every month when they pay the rent, you earn an income.

The average person struggling to make ends meet might not be able to purchase a building or write and successfully market a book. So how does one get to the point where they create some "pajama money"? Bear in mind that I am not a financial planner or advisor, I am merely sharing with you my experience and what has worked for me in the past and is currently working for me.

I've looked at scores of business models throughout my career, and one of the fastest ways to go from the basement to the balcony is Network Marketing. There are dozens of great Network Marketing companies out there. Take the time to do the research, go to their meetings, and see which one fits you best. Network Marketing is one of the simplest and fastest vehicles that will take the average American out of debt and towards financial independence. Keep in mind that marketing is governed by the same laws that govern the Universe. You can only get out of it, what you put into it. Simply speaking, it works if you work it.

The income initially generated from network marketing is not passive; you have to go out and earn it, but as you network with other marketers, you begin to receive a percentage of their efforts. Remember that it was billionaire and oil tycoon J. Paul Getty who said, "I would rather earn one percent of 100 people's effort than 100 percent of my own."

Since your time here is limited, it makes sense to leverage other people's time in your quest for wealth. The shortest and best way to make a fortune is to let people see clearly that it is in their best interest to promote yours, and that is what network marketing does. Since everyone is on the same page, promoting your interest is the same as promoting their interest.

This chapter was not written to sell you on all the wonderful things about network marketing; after all, it certainly isn't for everyone. I intend to give you other ways and vehicles to create wealth besides a regular job. I just don't believe that a nine to five is a viable means of achieving financial security.

As you increase your financial IQ and your wealth, be sure to keep it all in perspective. Do not allow your ego to get the best of you now that your standard of living has stepped up a notch. Pride goeth before destruction. Remain humble; remember that money is your servant, and it is your intention behind how you manage your money that makes it good or evil. Use your wealth and your resources to bring more joy into the world and the lives of your friends and family.

The reason I've included a chapter on money is that some of the most difficult challenges that I faced in life had to do with my relationship with money and my underlying feelings of unworthiness. I want the best for you; I want to see you happy, healthy, abundant, and prosperous.

When I lacked dollars, I was treated like garbage, especially in instances where I had a Sickle Cell crisis and visited some medical facility without having the adequate insurance coverage that I needed. Some might even go as far as saying that friends walked away from me, but that is not an accurate statement. Hard times never cause us to lose real friends; hard times simply reveal who your true friends are. So my wish is that from reading this book, not only will you lead a more fulfilling life, but also you will be more kind and compassionate with those who are still trying to find their path or are struggling along the way.

Be kind, gentle, and generous in all that you do, and the Law of Karma will work wonders in your life. You will not only be rich in dollars, but you will be one of the fortunate souls that are also rich in spirit. Please be sure to visit my website www.kirknugent.com for more strategies that you can implement to increase your abundance. I believe that in today's economy, money is necessary to create the freedom that we desire. I am currently teaching entrepreneurship to inner-city kids and helping them create a viable income. If you would like to learn how you can create an additional income via the internet, please email me at kirk@kirknugent.com, and I will assist you in making that dream a reality.

And finally, your consciousness surrounding money is a direct reflection of your thoughts and ideas surrounding yourself. In 2012, I was forced to pause and take inventory of my life. I realized that I was holding on to the idea that I was not worthy of love. Subconsciously, I had an old tape of childhood programming playing in my head, telling me that I was undeserving. Until I addressed that issue, money and all things good avoided me. Until you do the mental work and prepare your mind to receive money, you will not be able to keep and enjoy money. Your physical reality is a reflection of what's going on mentally. If you lack money, the problem is never money; the problem is always your ideas surrounding money. 'Change your mind, and you will change your life' is more than a cliché; it is the gospel.

CHAPTER 8

THE ANSWER IS ALWAYS LOVE

> "The Love that you withhold,
> is the pain that you will carry."
> *Alex Collier*

You get what you give. This is such a simple premise that most people miss the fact that it is also a Law that permeates the Universe. What we always have to be mindful of is the fact that if we are offering thoughts of fear, thoughts of doubt, thoughts or worry, and lack, then in return, we get situations where we are fearful. Situations where we are doubtful, where we are troubled, and indeed, we will find ourselves surrounded by an abundance of lack.

However, if we place our thoughts upon what we are grateful for, then we'll start attracting more things that fill us with gratitude. I remember a time in my life when I was struggling to keep the utilities on; I had five past-due letters from all of my utility companies, and they had already shut the cable off. I had no idea how I could turn the situation around because I didn't "see" any money in my immediate future.

I decided that I would do the only thing that I could do, and what I mean by that is I shifted my focus. If I found a penny on the floor, I would snatch it up, get really excited, and shout, "Wow, look at all this abundance that I found."

My son thought that was the silliest thing he'd ever seen, someone getting excited over a penny, so he started mimicking me. Whenever he found a penny, he would jump for joy, and we would celebrate the penny and place it in a jar of pennies that I called "Abundance."

He would come running home from school, "Hey dad, I found a nickel, let's put that with the other abundance."

How the bills got paid, I cannot tell you; I just know that they did, and none of our utilities were disconnected. Simply by being in a constant state of gratitude, I began attracting more to be grateful for, such as the electric company granting us an extension, or someone who owed me money that I forgot about decided to re-pay me. I had a series of small miracles that proved that an attitude of gratitude has the power to create magic in one's life.

I was getting good at mastering the art of being in a perpetual state of love and gratitude; however, I noticed that the definition of love gets very blurred and murky when I am in a relationship. The demands and expectations that we bring into a relationship destroy the very thing that we are seeking from the relationship. The dictionary defines love as a strong affection for someone, but I think such a definition is very limited and incomplete.

A complete description of love is found in the Bible. It tells us that love is patient, and love is kind. It does not envy; it does not boast; it is not proud. It is not rude, it is not self-seeking, it is not easily angered, and it keeps no record of wrongs. Love does not delight in evil but rejoices with the truth. It always protects, always trusts, always hope, and always perseveres. Love never fails. 1 Corinthians 13:4-8

Not only does this verse tell us what love is, but it also tells us what love is not. More often than not, we find relationships that are supposed to be loving, void of most of the qualities of what love is, and filled with what love is not. Our ability to give and receive love seems to be wrapped in ignorance and is nothing more than an extension of our insecurities. How many times have we met someone who claimed to love us and the minute that we get involved in a loving relationship, they do everything in their power to change us into who they believe we ought to be? In other words, who you are at this moment is not good enough, certainly not loveable.

"Honey, you can't wear that skirt; it is not long enough, you're with me now."

"Make sure you're home by ten; I don't want to have to wait up for you."

"What do you mean you want to stay up and watch a movie? Let's go to bed;

you're in a relationship now."

"Baby, you need to start losing some weight, you weren't this big when we met."

So the way we do love on this planet is not about the person that we claim to love, but rather it's about how well they can help to boost our egos and cover our insecurities. Our relationships are more about ownership than they are about relating to each other in a manner that is loving and free of judgments.

Wayne Dyer's definition of love seems to be more in alignment with Source's definition of love. Dr. Dyer uses the word Source to represent the same idea that religion uses to represent God. However, if that doesn't resonate with you, please feel free to substitute Source with God, Universe, Creator, Christ, Buddha, Allah, Jehovah, Consciousness, I AM that I AM or whatever feels best to your Being.

According to Dr. Dyer, "Love is the ability and willingness to allow those that you care for to be what they choose for themselves without any insistence that they satisfy you." In other words, allowing an individual to evolve at his pace and rate.

We are so loved and supported by Source that even if we believe that we are not loved and supported by Source, our reality reflects that belief. It's just another way of saying, "Whatever you believe to be true, whether that idea is loving or unloving, I will support you enough in that belief to reflect it to you in your reality." Source never insists, it never judges, it is not self-seeking, it merely observes and reflects that observation to us so that we can decide to make adjustments if what we are seeing is not to our liking.

Unfortunately, we seldom pay attention; we've forgotten who we are and what we are. We've been programmed to believe that conditional love is as good as it gets. The irony to that belief is, if it is conditional, it is not love. But we've invested so much in the idea of conditional love and a conditionally loving God that the closest we allow ourselves to come to the concept of receiving unconditional love is from a pet, usually a dog.

We are hard on each other because we are hard on ourselves. Using the Bible's definition of love, we generally do not deal with ourselves in a patient or kind manner. How many times when something goes wrong do we lash out at ourselves with things like, "Oh, I'm so stupid; I can't believe I did something so dumb… AGAIN!!"?

Until we learn to love the Being that we are unconditionally, it is highly unlikely that we can extend such a love to another person. Until we learn to love the skin that we are in, and the body that we are in, we will always respond to our reflection in an unloving manner.

The programs that we receive daily reinforce the idea that we are unworthy of love. A man who is the pastor of one of the largest congregations here in the United States posted on his Facebook page the following quote, "When we didn't deserve it when we made mistakes, God showed us his unconditional love..." The problem with his statement is the idea that love has to be earned, that somehow we are unworthy and could actually be undeserving of love. Ironically it is when someone is acting in an unloving manner that they're most in need of love.

If we are subconsciously coming from a place where we believe that we have to do something to be deserving of love, then we are always at the mercy of being manipulated by the person from whom we are seeking love. One unkind word from such a person can send our self-esteem to the basement. Based on their judgments and their tendency to withhold love from us, we, in turn, begin to withhold love from ourselves.

I believe that it makes more sense to walk through this world as light as possible, meaning walking through the world in a state of awe and observation rather than in a state of perpetual judgment. Whenever I am hard on myself, I notice that I am also hard on others and that my life spirals into a very negative flow within a short period. In other words, the harder I am on me, the harder my life becomes. However, the reverse is also true; the gentler that I am on myself, the more compassion the world seems to display towards me.

I am committed to showing up as authentic as possible, naked, and unashamed. If the world chooses to judge me, then so be it. But I refuse to walk around wearing a mask, simply because I've had a few experiences which served to foster my growth (well actually more than a few.... awe damn it, I did say naked and unashamed didn't I?). Ok, so I've had a WHOLE LOT of experiences. Ok, there, I said it, now Kirk, take a deep breath, have yourself a "Whooosaah" moment and get back to writing.

If you need a permission slip to stop judging yourself; to start being more gentle with yourself and others, consider this book your permission slip. Forget what others think; forget who you believe you are here to please; as such a person doesn't exist. You made that up. When you were created, no one said to you, "OK listen honey, now that you're on Earth, your purpose is to please Kirk Nugent, he is very wise, he knows more than you, he's an authority figure, and if you want his love you have to earn it because God knows you're undeserving."

No one said that; however, we've picked up that message along the way (which is bad), and somehow we've turned that twisted message into our personal truth (which is even worse for our spiritual growth). The more you start caring about how you feel as opposed to how others feel about you, the more you can shed the layers of the mask that don't serve you. There is nothing that you have to do to be deserving of love. Let the people who love you, love you, as you are; take you as you are, or leave you alone. You are a work in progress, be OK with that.

Please understand that this is not a permission slip to show up as an insensitive, narcissistic and manipulative person, but rather a permission slip to be gentle on yourself while you work on being the most authentic, loving and compassionate person that you are capable of being. Understand that you can never be authentic, loving, and compassionate with another person until you are that way with yourself. The kinder you are with yourself, the more understanding you will be when you meet a troubled soul along the way who is merely trying to find their path and reflect their frustration back at the world.

The people in our lives are usually there to reflect the areas in our lives in which we need to grow and also the areas in which we have grown. Their negative judgment of you doesn't have to be your condemnation of yourself, even if what they are sharing with you is uncomfortable. Chances are it is uncomfortable because a part of you identifies with that message.

For example, if someone said to me, "Kirk, you are a big fat slob." The only emotion that would be triggered within me is probably laughter because I know that I am having a one on one with someone who is off their meds. No part of me identifies with being a fat slob, not with the amount of sexiness that I bring to the table. Such a statement just wouldn't compute. However, if they said to me, "Kirk Nugent, you are on stage giving all this advice, encouraging people to ask for help when they need it, yet I don't see you asking for help when you need it. You wear a mask, just like everybody else." Such a statement would very likely trigger some negative emotional response because somewhere inside of me, I identify with being afraid to ask; somewhere inside of me, I have identified with being unworthy.

So even if what is being said is uncomfortable, such discomfort more often than not is a signal, or a sign from the Universe saying, "Get ready baby, I'm bringing you another opportunity to heal. You can thank me later after you're done being pissed at the messenger."

In every situation, life is there as a teacher, and we've all learned some very challenging and painful lessons. If you're willing to acknowledge that every person and every situation is an opportunity to heal, or a chance to integrate more fully the various aspects of yourself that you've left behind, or swept under the rug. If you make a conscious, deliberate decision to welcome all as teachers, then you can also request the Universe (Source, God, Batman, whatever you choose to call that power), that you wish to learn your lesson in a very gentle manner because you're now paying attention, and you are willing to leave the judgment behind because it no longer serves you.

I've found that approaching every situation with an open heart and with love softens the situation and makes it more palatable. I've found myself laughing at things that generally would 'make' me angry. It all depends on the lens that you are viewing the situation through. Choose love, regardless of the question; the answer is always love.

The Ultimate Answer

There was a time when all I wrote about was police brutality

There was a time when I picked up the pen

And rebelled against the sins of society,

My mission was to tear down this dynasty,

I was just sick of the hypocrisy.

These punk politicians who kept jacking me,

Kept playing us like they're so wise

And all I wanted to do was write the words

To bring about their untimely demise.

My pen spoke in violent tones

As I slaughtered them on the microphone.

But it's been a while since I've written with such anger

Because spiritually I'm growing much stronger,

And the smoke and mirror that has been placed in front of humanity

Is no longer real to me.

The illusions; no longer my reality.

Now I have Jamaicans walking up to me,

Saying, "I remember when you used to speak

Out against the unpopular truth."

"That was deep my youth.

But it's like now you've gone soft on me

All you want to write about is spirituality."

But I've observed this world of ours

And found that it's all vanity.

It's all an illusion to keep us vibrating

On this lower reality.

And whatever I give my attention to

Will eventually manifest

So from this day forth

God as my witness, I will only give my best.

I am not concerned about the productivity of your oil fields

But I'm concern about the pain that this child feels

From your backdoor Congressional deals.

I'm concern when this soldier bleeds,

And why is it that on CNN the story of the lowest vibration always leads?

When the bombs drop, who takes care of the needs of the refugees?

Who will deliver hope and empathy to the ones who have to flee?

Lord, I just want to be a better person in this society

I want to write the words that bring peace to humanity

Because once again in my life I'm having a moment of clarity

And between the physical and the spiritual, I'm here to bridge the disparity.

But where do I find the words to remind a sleeping nation that we're all one?

And how can I explain to an extremist that would kill me in the name of Allah

That, "Dude, I AM YOUR BROTHER!"

How do I explain to these appointed leaders

That if you're a leader, then by God, go ahead and lead.

But understand that you can never bomb for peace

And Capital punishment can never avenge the deceased.

Are there words that can remove generations of hate

Coursing through religious DNA?

To people who bow down and say,

"To the God of Abraham, I am Yours, and You are mine."

How do I let them know that Israel is no more sacred than Palestine,

And your geographical location doesn't necessarily make you divine,

But religious arrogance will indeed

Make you blind to the divinity of all mankind.

How do I explain to that young Islamic brother

Who is gunning for martyrdom

He's strapped with C4, shrapnel and then some,

About to board that Israeli bus

Because he's been programmed to think that doing this is a must

In order to immediately get to Paradise

And enjoy the services of seventy-two virgins in the afterlife.

How do I explain that it is all in vain?

How do you bring sanity to a nation that's gone insane?

How do you explain that there's an unseen hand exploiting our differences,

And we're falling for it.

We're now oblivious to the fruits of the spirit,

At one point we used to speak hate, now we live it!

So I watch every group praying to a different God

Who is allegedly up above

And His wavering philosophy seems to conform to their ideology like a glove

And they all seem to miss the point

That the answer is always LOVE!

CHAPTER 9

WHEREVER YOU GO, THERE YOU ARE

> "I keep preaching: Life is a mirror, that's all it is
> This world may be a stage, but this ain't no show biz.
> And if you can't grasp the concept that thoughts
> eventually manifest,
> Then that mirror called Life has a tendency
> to be merciless."
> Excerpt from my book,
> Answer The Call.

After traveling the planet for more than a decade, encouraging all who I've come in contact with to pursue their passion, and enjoy their lives to the fullest, I found my life quickly dismantling before my eyes in May of 2012. By June of 2012, I was feeling hopeless; there was a lingering sadness in my soul that would hold my heart hostage for the next six months.

I was living in beautiful West Palm Beach, Florida, and in an attempt to get as far away as possible from what I considered to be the source of my pain, I got in my car and drove to California to regroup. Spiritually I was aware that I could never outrun a challenge or a situation that my soul has brought to the surface to be addressed. However, my ego needed to be as far away from Florida as possible.

Upon my arrival in California, I searched Craigslist for a place to live. I was able to rent a room in someone's home, and now it was time to either get busy living or get busy dying. The living part did not appeal to me much. I was just tired of the lies, the hypocrisy and nonsense that life had to offer. I wasn't suicidal, but I was undoubtedly indifferent to what my future held.

My son was able to sense that I was in a dark place, a much darker place than he had ever experienced his eternally optimistic dad to be in. He would call, and at times spend four hours per day on the phone with me, giving me a pep talk. I guess he could tell that I needed a more compelling reason to remain on the planet, so he started telling me that he's going to need some help with college and other goals. I knew my son didn't need me in that sense, but I also realized that he didn't want me to leave, so it was time to find a way to pick up the pieces.

To make that happen, I would first have to ask myself some tough questions and be willing to answer those questions sincerely. I sat on the twin mattress that came with the room that I rented and surveyed my living quarters. Except for my car, parked in the driveway, and my collections of books in a storage facility in Florida, just about everything I owned was in that room with me. I felt like a fraud and a failure. Who am I to be telling anyone to pursue their passion, when I'm a total loser? I just could not muster the strength to look at how pathetic my life was.

The next month I had a performance at Central Michigan University, my favorite school in the world. I was looking forward to the love that I would get there; I needed the love that they gave me. This would be my twelfth time performing there in as many years.

They loved me, and I loved them, it was a necessary ego boost. Unfortunately, you can't hide from your issues, and until they've been honestly addressed, you simply cannot leave them behind. I got in my car and drove across the country to Mount Pleasant, Michigan. When I packed to leave California, among my necessities, I packed my sense of unworthiness with me. I kept the feeling that I was unworthy of love securely tucked away in my chest cavity as I set out to Central Michigan.

It was by far one of the worst performances of my life; I forgot my lines to poems I could typically do in my sleep. My mind just could not focus, and I felt as though I did a horrible job engaging the students. I walked off the stage, feeling more undeserving than before. The idea that I was a fraud and did not belong on that stage was fully awakened within me. To make matters worse, speaking was my life, and if I couldn't perform on stage, I had no reason for being. At least, that's what I thought at that moment.

Dani Hiar, the director of the Leadership program at Central Michigan, has a great love for me, and without a doubt, I have a great love for her. She could tell that something was amiss; after all, she's been booking me for twelve years, and I've never missed a line. I pride myself on my ability to deliver. I'm Kirk Nugent baby; I can move any crowd, just not this one, and not today. Dani sensed how low I was feeling and came over to encourage me. With great empathy and compassion, she expressed that she understood how badly I must feel but told me not to worry about it. "We will see you next year Kirk," she said. I could not believe that she would even entertain the thought of booking me for the thirteenth year; I certainly did not deserve to return to the great CMU stage.

I exited Central Michigan's auditorium, with my head hung low; I slowly made my way to my car. I got in, started the engine, and then the million-dollar question hit me, "Where are you going, Kirk?" Wow, I honestly didn't know. I was unable to answer the question, and it didn't matter whether it was being asked in a literal manner or figurative sense. You see, I gave up my room in California when I left for Michigan, so basically, I did not have an address. Yes, Kirk, Mr. Pursue Your Passion, you are once again homeless.

Yup, whether you want to or not, it's time to ask and answer those dreadful questions. Time to go within, because if you don't go within, you will always go without, and Kirk, my boy, you are basically without. Without a home, without love, without hope, without joy. Go within and live, evade the questions, and perish. Those are your options, so choose wisely.

Before I could answer, "Where am I going?" I needed to find out, "How did I get here?" A question that my ego was delighted to answer. "How did we get here? I will tell you how we got here. It was that Jezebel that you trusted, you gave her and her ungrateful, undisciplined kids everything that you had, and when you had no more, she cheated on you and left you for another man who was making more money than you. That's how we got here. Loving her was your most exquisite form of self-destruction. That's how we got here, end of story. What else do you want to talk about?"

I realized that on the surface, that's precisely how it appeared that my life unfolded, but I was also spiritually aware that whenever you remove responsibility from yourself, your equation and your life will always be unbalanced. It is the ego's job to make us feel good, so it makes sense that the ego will cast us as a helpless innocent victim. So the ego will tell you, "Yes, it was that 'Jezebel.' You had no role in attracting her, no part in allowing what transpired, no part in overlooking all the warning signs and absolutely no role in choosing the good that you deserve."

If I wanted any real and substantial change in my life, I had to go below the surface; I had to connect the dots and find my role in this situation. So I started doing what I do best, talk to myself. "OK Kirk, how did you get here? You are brilliant enough to figure this thing out, so figure it out so that we don't have to revisit this dreadful place anymore." I immediately began setting the intention for how I wanted my life to unfold.

Listen Life; I know that this sojourn is nothing but a series of lessons, and from this day forth, I want to learn my lessons in a gentle fashion, and in a loving manner, and no more do I choose to learn through pain. Can we agree on that? I also understand that physical reality is a mirror; it only reflects that which is taking place in my inner world, my thoughts, and my feelings towards myself and the world.

I believe that there's a Law of Karma; what I give out is what I get back. What I sow is what I reap. So I don't understand how I am faithful, but then my partner abandons me. Not only did she abandon me, but she left when I was at my lowest point. I don't see where I am sowing those seeds. I loved her, but it has become painfully obvious that she didn't love me. How am I sowing love and reaping betrayal? I don't get it, help me to understand. I know the lesson repeats until the lesson is learned, and I keep ending up in this same classroom, only with more callous teachers. I'm tired of repeating these same lessons; I'm tired, I don't know what else to do. I GIVE UP (in other words, I surrender). I surrender.

I started the car and headed east. I was going to New Jersey to see my son. I needed to see someone who loved me unconditionally, the person who would believe in me even when I didn't have to courage to believe in myself. New Jersey was a 13-hour drive, after driving for six, I checked into a hotel in Pennsylvania and decided to continue my journey in the morning.

Exhausted from my performance on stage, the weight of my world, and the hollow place in my soul, I collapsed on the bed and fell asleep. I woke up hours later, still feeling that perpetual emptiness in my soul and still pondering the question, "How did I get here?" I wasn't angry at my ex, it took me a couple of months to go through the entire DABDA* grief process, and thank God I was finally at acceptance. However, I knew that if I didn't correctly answer that million-dollar question, it was only a matter of time before I would find myself in a similar, yet more devastating situation.

*The "Five Stages of Grief" are now almost universally applied to the emotional reactions that follow a significant loss. The stages are typically defined as Denial, Anger, Bargaining, Depression, and Acceptance, or DABDA.

'Until you make the unconscious conscious, it will direct your life, and you will call it fate. -- Carl.G. Jung.

It wasn't long before I heard that voice; the voice that I had come to recognize as my 'Higher Self' was now responding to my inquiry. "Yes Kirk, you can only get what you give; you can only reap what you've sown. Physical reality is merely a reflection of your inner world, and you are the constant variable in that world. Yes, your ex abandoned you, but only after you abandoned yourself by harboring these childhood feelings of unworthiness. Yes, she left when debts were high, and the funds were low, but isn't that what you do Kirk? Your self-worth is so intimately entwined with your financial worth that the minute your finances become constipated, so does the love and value that you place on yourself. You are the first to betray the value that you've placed on yourself when things are tight. You are the first to walk away from feeling good about yourself; you are the first to doubt yourself. Your former lover only reflected to you the thoughts that you secretly harbored about yourself. You can't hide from who you are Kirk, because wherever you go, there you are, and the lesson repeats until the lesson is learned.

You've been down this road before, but you've never adequately addressed the problem of you not loving yourself. So once again, you find yourself in the classroom of Life, with the same teacher dressed in a different face. When you avoid loving yourself, the Universe will keep on sending you people who will also avoid loving you. It is holding up a mirror for you to see yourself and make the necessary adjustments."

The mirror of relationships always reflects to us, those areas of ourselves that we tend to tuck away in the back of the closet. It reflects those areas that we avoid consciously looking at, and those areas will be brought to the surface through our relationships so that they may be healed. Our greatest lessons always come from our most intimate relationships, so yes Kirk, your ex was out of integrity, but only after you stepped out of integrity with who you know yourself to be, an aspect of the Divine. The quality of the love that you receive will always reflect the value that you place on yourself. All of your pain, all of your difficulties, and all of the suffering that you have experienced came from your attempt to manipulate the mirror instead of changing who you are.

Slowly I started nodding my head in agreement, "Yeah, I get it... I get it. But I don't want to end up back here. I'm tired of being in relationships where I am the last one to know that it has ended. How do I fix this?"

"It's simple Kirk, love yourself, and value yourself. It's been a while since you've loved and valued you. You're still walking around playing back these messages of unworthiness that were fed to you by your parents during your childhood. It's time to bring these messages to the Light and allow them to heal. It's time for you to know that the Universe is one of order, and there are no accidents. Your parents were the perfect teachers to prepare you for the role that you chose.

You've forgiven them; don't you think it's time to forgive yourself? You are a child of the Divine, don't believe that; KNOW THAT!" Remember the words of the Master Jesus, "Don't you know, ye are GODS, and all of you are children of the Most High?"

"Kirk, Life is like a grindstone; it will either polish you or pulverize you. It all depends on how you position yourself. You can take your experiences, and you can become bitter, or you can become better, the choice is yours. So many men take the experience of one broken heart, and they use that experience to punish every woman that they subsequently meet. Be better Kirk, be better, and use this experience to approach the world with a more open heart, have love and compassion for the people that you meet. Remember, people who have been hurt usually hurt others. Healed people help others to heal. Be the Light that you were created to be, let the world see a smile shining through all those years of pain, let yours be a life of inspiration for all who you meet, you are too big to be bitter, too special to be spiteful and too great to hold a grudge. Remember that sometimes we are taken into troubled waters not to drown but to be cleansed, we will be bent, but not broken, shaken but not shattered, discouraged but not defeated.

So the same goes for you. Yes, you who are reading these words, you are a child of the Divine, and you have the ability to rearrange every aspect of your life and mold it into whatever you desire. However, having the ability to do something and doing it are two separate entities. With a burning desire to control your destiny and a focused intention on the desired outcome, brick by brick, you can rebuild the very foundation of your life. Your thoughts are very creative, so lift your thoughts out of the gutter of self-pity and into the majestic realms of self-empowerment.

I made a conscious decision very early in life that I would take total responsibility for everything that happened in my life. There are no accidents, and I am the constant variable in the equation of my life. Those words sound great, but often ego and emotion get in the way. Sometimes it feels good (in a sadistic kind of way) to be the victim. Our ego loves to tell the story of how we were so innocent, and everybody did us wrong. That's a great way to live for the ego, but a terrible existence for a self-empowered being.

Several years ago, I had another "failed" relationship. I put the word failed in quotations because relationships cannot fail. The real purpose of a relationship (any relationship) is for each individual in the relationship to allow the other to discover how to be more of who they truly are, and vice versa. So relationships will always bring things to the surface for us to examine, for us to make a decision regarding what we do and do not prefer, and determine what is a vibrational match for our frequency at that time and what isn't. Unfortunately, most people have no idea of the real purpose of relationships and, therefore, distort it into some perverse form of ownership.

I digress; several years ago, I had what I believed to be a failed relationship. It ended very bitterly, and we went our separate ways, basically despising the very existence of each other. After about six months, I decided that I didn't want this negative energy in my life, my ego wasn't as engaged as it was six months prior and I'm a rather forgiving person. I called my former girlfriend and requested a face to face meeting. She told me that she was surprised that I called, and she figured that based on her previous actions that I would never speak to her again.

When we sat down, I explained to her that I totally understood how we got to such a place of bitterness and resentment, and I also want to acknowledge what my role was in the situation.

I told her, "Please listen for a second, I want to talk to you, but I don't want to speak to your ego, I left my ego in the car so that my Higher-Self could speak to your Higher-Self, no judgments, just a clearing of the air."

Her poker face gave way to her astonished expression as she nodded, "OK."

"I know that when we met, you loved me in the purest way possible. You constantly gave me love. However, nothing you did was ever good enough. I keep requiring more from you for me to love you in the manner that you loved me, it only made sense that after a while your hurt would turn into anger, and you would lash out. I get that now. What I want you to understand is something that I'm just beginning to understand. It wasn't you who I was rejecting but rather myself (subconsciously), I never believed that I was worthy of love, so, therefore, it was impossible for me to accept it from you, and being that I had no love for myself, I certainly had none to give to you. I'm saying this because I know you felt guilty for what went down between us, but I don't want you to look at it that way. See it as a learning experience; we are both older and wiser. I judged you very harshly, but now it has become painfully obvious that every time that I judge someone else, I am revealing an unhealed part of myself. Until I start loving me, I'll never be able to love another, so go in peace knowing that I forgive you, and I've forgiven myself."

I watched the tears roll down her cheeks, "Kirk, I've always loved you. I don't know what they did to you in your childhood, but your heart was so inaccessible. All I ever wanted was for you to love me. I'm glad we had this talk; I forgive you as well, and I love you. I hope one day you'll find whatever you're searching for. You are a beautiful soul Kirk; you deserve love, and it will keep seeking you out, accept it."

Once we put our ego aside and come together from a place of love and understanding, life tends to smooth itself out. Set the intention for your life; choose not to invalidate the other person's perspective and then deal from a place of compassion. A drama-free life is the beginning of an abundant life. Engage the world from a place of love. Choose to see the beauty all around, and to walk away from the stuff that doesn't serve you. Choose to go in peace, and you will see every area of your life improve. Your health will be better, your peace of mind will improve, and you will enjoy a more restful sleep with more pleasant dreams. This life is always about your choices, never about chance.

Here's something to help you remember who you are and to also put your world in perspective. I got it from a beautiful musician and brother in Australia, Amir Paiss. He taught me that we are made of love. Begin repeating to yourself, whenever you're alone or when you're going about your day, the mantra, "We are made of love, we are made of love." Act accordingly, go about your day knowing that you are divinely loved, adored, and cared for. When you come in contact with one who is having a difficult time in their journey, remind yourself that this individual is also made of love. Love is who you are, so be love. Be at peace, be anxious for nothing

I want to leave you with a very healing exercise that I did. If you find it to be of value to you, then try it. I wrote a letter to my former self, the scared little kid inside of me that was traumatized by years of abuse from parents who lacked the tools (at the time) to deal with their trauma.

A Letter to My Former Self

Beloved Kirk,

Look at you. You've been on this Earth for almost a decade now, and it hasn't been a lovely ride so far, has it? I gaze into your eyes only to find deep-reaching sorrow, an absence of joy. You're not even ten as yet, and already you've allowed life to extinguish your will to live. You are so depressed that you won't eat, you're not even 80 pounds, pure skin, and bones. Your caregivers are unaware of what you're feeling, what you are dealing with. They're oblivious to your pain and indifferent to your hurt.

The words of your father keep ringing in your ear, "Why can't you just die? I watch the news, and I see a school bus crash, and kids die. Why the f*ck can't you just die?"

You lay awake in bed at night in total darkness, and you playback your mother's words, "I don't know why God didn't just kill me instead of making me bring something like you into this world."

I know, you lack the words to articulate what you're feeling, but deep down, you know that you are unloved and unwanted. You feel as though you are nothing but a financial burden to your parents, and you eagerly await your doctor's death sentence. They promised you that because of the severity and ravaging effects of Sickle Cell Anemia on your body and internal organs, you would probably be dead by the age of 13. That prognosis is your only flicker of hope. I get it, soon you will be gone, you will no longer be a burden to anyone, and your parents can live happily ever after. After all, you just want your parents to be happy, and it seems as if your existence robs them of their joy.

Well kid, I've got news for you. You see, I am you, 30 years into the future. So obviously you did not die, you did not perish. Instead, you defied the odds, and you will continue to defy the odds in just about every area of your life. In six years, you are going to become obsessed with books and reading. Yes, (Haha, even more, obsessed than you are now). By the age of 25, you will have bought and read over 1,000 books, and for some strange reason, you will sign all of your books: "Kirk Nugent, Born to Win, Destined to be Great."

As unaware as you currently are of the power of the spoken words, you will speak the idea of, "Kirk Nugent born to win, destined to be great" into existence. Your words will become flesh. Your shy little ass, which refuses to make eye contact and can barely speak above a whisper in public, will become... (wait for it). Kirk, you're going to become a public speaker, not just a public speaker, but an inspirational speaker and a damn good one (if I may say so myself). You will speak in arenas in front of thousands of people at a time, moving them to tears, inspiring them to pursue their passion. They will hang on to your every word; they will purchase your books and download your mp3 audio files from the internet. (Oh BTW, the mp3 and internet thing hasn't been invented as yet, but what I'm saying is that you're doing great work). People will follow you on Twitter, Facebook, Instagram, and YouTube (yeah more future technologies) anyway, you get the picture.

Dude, do you remember when you had a Sickle Cell crisis and missed two months of school in Mrs. Hylton's 5th-grade class? Do you remember how happy you were when you returned and realized that you missed an assignment to write a poem because you just KNEW that you could never write anything as good as what the other kids wrote? You might want to sit down for this one Kirk. Son, you are a poet, a real-life, walking, talking inspirational poet! People will pay thousands of dollars for you to fly all over the world so that you can perform one of your poems. They will fly you to Australia, The Netherlands, India, Hong Kong, Canada, St. Croix, St. Thomas, The Bahamas, Puerto Rico, Jamaica (oh yeah, you live in Florida now). You will perform in every single state in the United States, and you are SEVERELY LOVED. But wait, there's more, it gets better.

You have a son that you love and adore, and he loves and adores you. Through his actions, you will learn to forgive all of this bullshit that you're going through now. Through his actions, he will teach you how to love unconditionally. Kirk, your life is about to be so sweet, one could become diabetic just by observing it (see, that's that poetic thing that you do that I'm talking about).

If I could give you one piece of advice, it would be to love yourself. Dude, you went damn near 40 years without loving you, now that's a damn shame son, a damn shame. Because you walked around with this deep-seated feeling of unworthiness, and not loving yourself, you attracted all kinds of crazy relationships. The people who didn't love you, you allowed in, and the ones who truly loved you, you sent packing. What kind of twisted shit is that Kirk? Fortunately for you, through all of those books that you read, you uncovered the secret of the Law of Attraction. Somewhere in your late 30's, you started to understand that life is a mirror, and it can only reflect you. So all changes begin within, and you were willing to take an in-depth look in the darkest places of your soul, and somehow you managed to bring that darkness into the Light. Frickin' genius kid; frickin' genius! So fear not Kirk, you fared very well.

I won't lie to you; the road will be rocky for a while, and many false friends will abandon you. Every time you gave a woman your heart, it was shattered and returned to you. You dealt with many betrayals from friends and family alike. You had some pain Kirk, some real legitimate pain. Oh, but you were not so innocent yourself, you built steel walls around your heart, so afraid of being hurt that you would rather strike first, and on many occasions you did. You're such a Scorpio, anyway kid; I'm here to let you know that you made it through the storm. You did well, you finally learned how to forgive, how to love, and equally important, how to allow. You learned how to let others be without any insistence that they please you. Kirk, you love deeply, and you are deeply loved. See you in about three decades.

Kirk Nugent

Born to Win,

Destined to be Great!

The whole purpose of this book is to remind you that nothing in your life can be so dead that a shift in perspective cannot resurrect it. When you look at everything that is unfolding in your life as a lesson for you to grow, to expand, to become fully integrated with all aspects of yourself, and when you take on the eyes of your creator, you will also take on the consciousness of your creator. That consciousness is also called the consciousness of Christ. Now, armed with that perspective, you can begin to add more life to your years, which in turn can add more years to your life. Go forth and live with purpose, make this one count, YOU ARE STILL HERE!

I intend to gently remind you of who you are and what you are. This Matrix that we live in tries its best to detract us from our greatness. Just about every program that is running in the Matrix encourages you to be timid and afraid. As we come to the end of this book, let me leave you with the following reminder, it's a poem that I wrote a little over a decade ago, but I want to dissect the poem so that you can walk away with a thorough appreciation of the magic that is you.

I Need You to Remember:

In regards to the title, I Need You Remember; I want you to think of your hand. Your hand consists of five fingers; each finger is also a member of the hand. If one of those fingers is detached from the hand, the hand cannot function as well as it was ultimately designed to function. In our own way, we've more or less detached from the hand of humanity, and we are programmed to see ourselves as separate from all creation. So whenever I ask you to remember, I am not only asking you to recall some information that you've buried deep within the subconscious mind, I am also asking you to re-join (re-member) the family of creation and once again be aligned with the whole. Let us be one, and therefore study war and division no more.

I've been three decades in the darkness,

Three decades in the wilderness

Three decades of amnesia,

And now I'm beginning to remember.

***I've been on this planet for 30 years, totally oblivious to who I AM,

but now I am beginning to wake up to the true nature of who I AM.

I know that you're thinking that we haven't met

Don't get too perplexed, but hear me before you step

When I say, "My God, you look familiar."

***I know that you think that we are strangers,

but I am now seeing that we are very much connected.

I am beginning to remember that we're born of Light

Created to shine long before infinity could tell time,

And we cannot be denied.

***I am beginning to remember our connection to God/All That Is/Source.

So now, I am beginning to shed this programming.

I am beginning to realize that these people that I hate

I don't really know them,

But it's the patriotic thing to do.

***I am beginning to realize that through the programming of the media and other news outlets, I am told who my enemies are,

even though I have no quarrels with anyone on this planet or any other planets.

So now I am beginning to move away from MANipulation

Towards self-actualization, towards wisdom and inner peace.

And the turbulence cease like an absence of the breeze,

And I'm really beginning to like this energy.

***I am beginning to think for myself, and because of that,

my stress level is significantly reduced.

I am beginning to realize that there is no separation between God and me

So now, I am beginning to be like the tree.

For no tree has branches so foolish as to fight among themselves,

And we're all branches of the same tree called humanity.

And I need you to remember.

***I am beginning to wake up to the fact that Source is ever-present, so there can never be a disconnect between my Source and myself, and if we are all connected to Source, then fighting another, would be the same as fighting myself.

Now I'm beginning to straighten my back,

Raise up off my knees,

My connection to sun, moon, and star

Get decreed, like I was Cherokee

Recognizing his oneness to Spirit

Outside of his tepee,

And for the first time in my life, I'm free!

***I am beginning to stand in my power and seeing my connection to everything.

Because of that, I can no longer be manipulated, and it feels good to be free.

How could I've been so shallow

As to wage war against my shadow?

Born of the same spirit, just different faces

But now I'm beginning to remember that

The fight is not against flesh and blood

But spiritual wickedness in high and low places.

***Now that I am awake, I'm amazed that we are so divided, but I also understand that 'division' is something we are taught very early in life from the programming that is all around us.

I am beginning to remember that my free-will cannot be bought,

I'm a member of the Ground Crew sent to stop the onslaught.

So no longer shall I major in victimology

Opposed to opportunity,

Not when I was born with the winning credentials,

A spirit that's celestial.

***I am beginning to wake up to the idea that when you stand in your power, you cannot be manipulated. I am waking up to the idea that if I get in tune with the Divine, I don't have to be a victim, and my example will, in turn, wake others.

So today I'm like a team of Army Rangers

Cause even though we're so-called strangers

Not one soul gets left behind.

So the question is

Can these bones live?

And without a shadow of a doubt

I assure you that the answer

Is 'Affirmative!'

***So no matter how 'lost' someone seems to be. Without a shadow of a doubt,

they will find their way back to Source. We are never disconnected; we have only forgotten our connection.

Oh, ye of little faith,

You were born to win

Destined to be great.

What comfort do you find

In these aches and pain?

Why do you endorse the crying game?

Why do you deny that you're a reflection of the Most High?

And why do you allow yourself to be manipulated into shame?

Come on, think. It's important that you remember!

***Why do we complain about the way things are, yet we corporate with it?

Why complain about your job, then turn around and go to that job the very next day?

For everything in our lives, we're responsible.

So beloved, is it possible,

That the reason we're dissatisfied with our conditions

Impatient with our solutions,

Is because we've been asking the wrong questions?

***We tend not to ask empowering questions,

therefore, most of our answers are disempowering.

Those who dance are considered insane

By those who can't hear the music.

And volunteer victims soon grow sick

Of a life that's all too basic.

You are light vibrating consciousness

So why do you choose to cooperate with this wickedness?

Why live your lives trying to please human beings

Who knows nothing about being human?

Because if they did, it would be understood

That the true meaning of compassion,

Is without ridicule, allowing a man to pursue his passion.

Without tyranny affording a woman the opportunity

To manifest her Destiny.

***When you choose to follow your heart, most people won't understand you, and that's OK.

If you are fed up with the mundane, then it might just be time for you to step into your magnificence.

To dream the impossible dream

To shoot for the moon and live among the stars.

Within the questions lie the answers

To all the concerns of your heart.

And it is critically important

That you find peace,

Long before you're deceased.

So forgive my intrusion, this mental fender bender

But now more than ever, I need you to remember.

They've rolled the dice so now your life is at stake

Whether you ride or die depends on your ability to stay awake,

AKA, your emotional maturity.

But without the questions, ladies and gentlemen, there can be no clarity.

*** You came here to dream bigger dreams and to live a more fulfilling life, but the airwaves are flooded with so much fear that we tend to surrender those dreams. However, it is critically important that you wake up to your real identity.

I'm talking about a commitment to total responsibility.

A lack thereof places your life in jeopardy,

But unlike Alex Trebek, today I'm giving you the questions.

Hopefully, they'll cut through the upholstery

Penetrate deep into the extrasensory

Like a brain on a treadmill, I'm trying to jog your memory

So help me help you escape this penitentiary.

***By taking 100% responsibility for your life and your attitude,

you will begin to stir the consciousness awake.

First question is:

Who's in charge of your destiny?

Can someone actually MAKE you mad

Or did you choose to linger in resentment?

Are you loving everything that you do,

Or is this the life that your parents prescribed for you?

Your job, is that your passion being manifested on the physical scene

Or are you just building someone else's dream?

Hope I didn't lose you

But within the answers to those questions

Lie the direct quality of your future.

So it is important that you remember.

***Introspection will help you escape the prison that has been constructed around your mind.

Do you really believe that someone else can complete you?

Or there is any human being above or beneath you?

Who besides yourself can break your heart?

Victor or victim, who chooses your path?

Everything is a choice, are you aware of that as yet?

Would you be mad at me if I told you that

No one can make you angry; you chose to be upset?

The challenges of life are here to make us better, not bitter.

Did you realize that everyone you encounter in life is your teacher?

To balance the equation, you become their teacher in turn

And the lesson repeats until the lesson is learned.

***Until you make the unconscious conscious, it will direct your life, and you will call it fate.

So who's in charge of your happiness?

Your loneliness, your emptiness?

Most of your worries are senseless

And someone else's opinion of you is none of your business.

Why do you choose to sing along with the given chorus?

What gives your life purpose?

When did you become so pacified

And what will it take for you to be satisfied?

***Consciousness awakens as we begin to look within and withdraw our attention from the programming that was given to us.

Do you know how much I love you?

Of course, not, can't tell you that,

What if you don't love me back?

I rather wait until you're lying in a mahogany box

Such a paradox.

But isn't that how the script is usually read?

So the question is,

Do you honor the living as passionately as you mourn the dead?

***Our insecurities keep us from fully awaking and experiencing all the deliciousness that life has to offer.

Remember when you would leap

And grow your wings on the way down?

What happened to that?

Remember when you used to live in the moment?

Of course not?

You were only two then,

And since then, you were trained to repress who you are!

Your sense of adventure,

But this poem wouldn't be so long

If it wasn't important that you remember.

***At what point did you stop having fun? What happened to make you no longer excited about this journey?

When was the last time you did something for the first time?

Better yet, how much quiet time do you set aside deprogram your mind?

Remove the blindfold and behold

You're so much more than you've been told.

You're like an emperor who chooses to panhandle

Like the sun believing it was a mere candle.

You were born blessed, never cursed

Yet you behave like the ocean dying of thirst.

But I can feel your spirit now,

You're tired; you want to put an end to all this illusion

Delusion, confusion, you want the chaos to cease.

You just want peace.

***Your Spirit is battle-weary; the emotional anguish from living in survival-mode has taken its toll.

So now you can no longer ignore

That voice in your core

Telling you that this life,

It just has to be about something more.

And just like you, I don't want any enemies,

I want to sit in the presence of a loving family

One called humanity,

Dipped in spirituality.

Where there are sense and sensibility.

But they're feeding us complexities

Stereotypes and warlike theories.

Oblivious of the fact that mentally

We're chained to slavery.

How could we be so blind?

This is the question that frustrates me.

***Finally, we have arrived at a time and place where consciousness refuses to remain asleep;

our soul is now forcing us to look at our world and make better choices.

But I guarantee you this,

If today we should refrain from spiritual suicide,

Starve the ego until it is deceased.

Then tonight, the genocide would cease.

Because just like it requires billions of pebbles

For a mountain to be constructed with ease.

So is world peace constructed by billions of souls with inner peace.

Now, do you understand why IT IS IMPORTANT THAT YOU REMEMBER?

***We cannot change the world until we change ourselves.

And that my friend is the key, when you change yourself, your world begins to change. Focus on being a new and improved version of yourself daily, don't be afraid of the parts of you that are lurking in the dark, that are coming up to heal. Embrace them with love and watch the world love and embrace you in turn. Remember the words of Rumi, "Your task is not to seek for love, but merely to seek and find all the barriers within yourself that you have built against it." Be gentle and compassionate with yourself and with others, because everyone you meet is your teacher and in every moment lies the opportunity for you to grow into your highest ideal. I believe in you, and I believe in that most magnificent Spirit that resides within you. Trust your heart and follow your passion. I believe there is greatness in you, and I challenge you not to settle for anything less.

Much Love.

Made in the USA
Columbia, SC
23 July 2022